ENVIRONMENTAL
THERAPY

MARTIN NORMAN

Environmental Therapy
Copyright © 2025 by Martin Norman

ISBN: 979-8894791401 (sc)
ISBN: 979-8894791418 (e)

All rights reserved. No part of this publication may be reproduced, distributed, or transmitted in any form or by any means, including photocopying, recording, or other electronic or mechanical methods, without the prior written permission of the publisher and/or the author, except in the case of brief quotations embodied in critical reviews and other noncommercial uses permitted by copyright law.

The views expressed in this book are solely those of the author and do not necessarily reflect the views of the publisher, and the publisher hereby disclaims any responsibility for them.

The Reading Glass Books
1-888-420-3050
www.readingglassbooks.com
fulfillment@readingglassbooks.com

CONTENTS

Introduction 1
Preparation 7
The Sea Landscapes 11
  Introduction 11
  Part One 12
- Using Rock Pools 12
- Lessening of their Sense of Responsibility 14
- The Shoreline 15
- Understanding Boundaries: The Sea Edge 16
- Developing a Sense of Identity: The Sand Castle 18
- Releasing Responsibility 19
- Affirmation: Rock Corridors 20
- The Sands: Safe Communication for the Child 21
- Releasing Stress and Anxiety 23
- The Stony Beach 26

  Part Two 28
- The Rocky Coastline: Processing Shock and Trauma: A Case Study: 28
- The Sandy Beach 31
- The Sheltered Cove 32
- Harbour Slipways 35
- Wild Beaches 36
- Returning to a Familiar Seascape 38
- Examples of how the Sea-shore can be used: 39

The Park Landscape 40
  Introduction 40
  Case Study One: Significance 41
- Introduction 41
- Restoration and Nurturing (Part One) 41

- (i) Managing Conflicting Emotions 44
- (ii) Expressing Reality 45
- Empowerment (Part Two) 46
- Understanding (Part Three) 49
- Expression (Part Four) 50

Conclusion 52

Case Study Two: Nurturing 52

Examples of how the park can be used: 60

Relevant Environments for the Child 62

Introduction 62

Case Study: Jack 63

- Introduction 63
- Familiar Landmarks 65
- The Cemetery (First Phase) 65
- The Ten-pin Bowling Centre 66
- The Family Inn (First Phase) 68
- The Cycle Trail (First Phase) 72
- The Family Inn (Second Phase) 73
- The Cemetery (Second Phase) 74
- The Family Inn (Third Phase) 75
- Listening to Music 75
- The Cycle Trail (Second Phase): 76
- Change of Focus 76
- Seeing His Father 77
- Moorland Peak 78
- Achieving his Goal 79
- Placing very challenging events in Perspective 80

Conclusion 82

Outdoor Development 84

Introduction 84

Three Case Studies 85

- Case Study One: Loss 85

- Case Study Two: Focus...90
- Case Study Three: Self Image 94

Conclusion 95

Using Animals in the Environment:..96

Introduction 96

- Case Study One: Belonging...98
- Model of Affect..106
- Case Study Two: Understanding................................107
- Case Study Three: Expression.....................................118

Thematic Understanding:..128

- Friendships 128
- Bullying..130
- Normality...133
- Nurturing...134
- Empowerment 137

Conclusion 139

Appendix One: Recognising the affect of abuse........................142

Bibliography 144

INTRODUCTION

The theoretical framework from which I come is person-centred, with the belief that it is my role to empower the client or young person to fulfill their true potential and find the deep resources within themselves, to know who they really are. To be able to reach this point of recognition, their locus of evaluation, can be a turning point in their lives, and then helping them to find their own emotional resources to achieve this i.e. to self-actualise, and move away from a negative self-concept, is core to this approach.

Often those young people who have experienced traumatic abuse, and have had to leave their immediate family, have a very negative self-concept, and lived or survived through learning to please their parents, and repressing their true feelings and expectations. This could leave them feeling very confused with conflicting emotions, not knowing who they really are i.e. their real identity, when in care or living with their wider family e.g. Grandparent.

Through having an opportunity to express how they feel in terms of what happened to them, and begin to understand this, they can then find the resources to move forward in their lives, through support and care. Nevertheless this can be a very hard process when they have felt so loyal to their family, and wish more than anything else to have been treated well by their parents and not by anyone else.

To seek to help them express the complexity of their lives, I have also used a creative model of counselling, using the natural environment alongside a person centred approach. This is based on my background in outdoor and environmental education, in which I have worked with young people both as a teacher and outdoor instructor, and seen how it both motivated them educationally, and also improved their self-confidence and emotional well being. After training as a counsellor, I found the combination of these three professional disciplines, in an outdoor context, had a powerful affect on the lives of young people, particularly if affected by trauma and abuse.

In that sense it is integrated too, and adopts methods using the natural environment which help the young person to feel both safe and accepted, and able to share their experiences in a way with which they can cope. This often applies sensory approaches using sounds, such as the waves of the sea, touch involving animals, or sight relating to turbulent natural scenes to symbolise what is too difficult initially to verbalise. This has often given them the emotional strength to trust the therapist and themselves, to talk about the most painful aspects of their lives, and understand how they have been affected.

Following this they are able then to distinguish their own self-view and what matters to them, and develop understanding of who they really are, which is the beginning of release from their traumatic past.

This book, as mentioned above, focuses on a creative approach, which I have used which is person or child centred, but which specifically focuses on the natural environment, and how I used different aspects of it creatively to reach young people, badly affected by abuse, neglect, and loss. This was through allowing them simply to be themselves. They had previously found it very hard to trust people and articulate their feelings, in any context, and engage with professional bodies.

The first three sections of this book deal with using different natural environments, chosen by the young person, to facilitate therapeutic engagement, and the fourth and fifth sections focus on outdoor development and the use of animals, therapeutically within the natural environment. Included in the third section, is also how indoor environments can be used therapeutically, to help the young person.

As mentioned above, there are considerable difficulties for the young person who has witnessed or experienced a traumatic background, through abuse and or neglect, and where there have been unclear 'guidelines' or boundaries concerning acceptable conduct between their parents and towards them, this leaves an uncertainty for them as to how they themselves should behave.

Often this can prove very difficult if the young person has had to go into care, and has to meet new standards of conduct, with which they themselves have to abide, within their foster or adoptive placement. These new standards both expected by their carers, and seen by the young person between their carers, can create a difference which both challenges what the young person has been used to, and can elicit feelings of anger that this is expected of them when the people they most love-their birth family have not been able to show this. Their pain and anguish can be considerable, and can lead to feelings of strong anger, that the very people-their foster or adoptive families who expect this of them, are not the people they would most wish this from, but their own birth mother and/or father.

This can lead to feelings of anger both with themselves if they feel they are to blame (for having to leave their family), or their own birth parents, which their carers may have to deal with. This may come alongside a very strong testing that they won't be let down again, and the only way to do this is to keep pushing limits, until they can really know this is the case. This can lead to very stressful situations between both the carers and the young person in their care.

Even where considerable care is shown along with affection and love to the young person, by their foster carers or adoptive parents, and is seen and appreciated by the young person, it can make it all the harder for them to accept, when this was not shown by their birth parents. They can therefore rebel from this, as it highlights for them the rejection they have felt from their own family, and the conflict involved.

This can also apply to grandparents of the young person whether maternal or paternal, who may be their new carers, and even though there is a family tie, it can still lead to the same sense of conflict for the young person, and testing reactions, where their sense of underlying loss and grief from their primary attachment figure (mother or father), or original sense of family togetherness, is not being replaced. This can lead to a sense of helplessness, which often needs an outlet through anger and/or aggression, or a deeper sense of withdrawal, if an avoidant attachment.

Their view of what is right and wrong can become very blurred or confused for them, when what they felt what was originally normal or acceptable behaviour when living in a traumatic and abusive background, and/or with neglect, or a deeper lifestyle sense that 'this is how it is', is challenged by their new carers. It can be a hard process for them to begin to recognise that their previous lifestyle was very wrong. Through this process they can begin to wonder about their own self, and who they really are, which can lead to a further expression of testing conduct standards alien to what they have been used to

At the same time this expression of individuality may be the beginnings of them finding themselves beyond their family background, and therefore the sometimes painful journey they and their carers face, has every opportunity to lead them to a place of understanding themselves of what is right and wrong, and being their own person. There is the opportunity for a very positive outcome.

The key aspect is to recognize that each child (Martin and Beezley, 1977) will have their own unique responses depending on their early life experiences and relationship with their birth family, and all are ways of coping, or learnt styles of interaction. Survival for the young person depends on how well the specific coping style fits the expectations of their birth parents. Therefore, it is understandable that it is very hard to unlearn this when in care. This also seems a key aspect for foster carers, adoptive parents, or family carers to be aware of. The view of the traumatised and abused child, is a distorted 'world view', but awareness of why it is so ingrained could be the benchmark for successful strategies and approaches, to change this, alongside understanding the affects of this compliance with their birth family, on their behaviour at home, or in school (please refer to appendix one).

I have found that environmental landscapes have been invaluable in allowing young people to express these conflicts and immense challenges in their lives, and begin to gain a sense of understanding of the importance of boundaries for themselves. The two landscapes, which have been most frequently chosen by young people I have worked with, are the Sea Landscape and Parks. However, equally environments linked to their early life e.g. their local town or village, or which they have identified with culturally e.g. a quiet family pub where they can play pool, or ten pin bowling have proved popular, alongside environments which offer a fresh stimulus for their future lives. The key aspect is allowing the child to choose the landscapes where they can most effectively be themselves.

Preparation

However, before visiting a sea or park environment (or any other outdoor environment), certain key preparations need to be made beforehand. It can be very helpful to consult colleagues in your team, of your thinking in terms of working outdoors, or what you hope to achieve, and their view of this beforehand, whether your manager, Social Worker, or other therapists. This also needs to apply to any indoor environments being used, in therapeutic work.

Because the therapist may be either lone working or out of the office for the day, it could also be valuable to keep in touch with colleagues regarding your location, or at least keeping colleagues involved through supervision, of the theme of work you are undertaking for a phase of time. This could allow a sense of connection for the therapist, that they are supported. Another option is letting a 'buddy' from your team know where you are going. If involved with children in care, or adoption letting the foster carers or adoptive parents know, your location, is really important, in case a problem arises. Linked to this having a mobile phone connection, is also essential.

A pre-visit is also necessary for any outdoor locations, for safety, and if a beach location for example, can allow potential hazards to be assessed, such as cliffs, rocks, or tide and mud. Also, the quality of access to the beach, or outdoor environment, is important. If this is properly researched, it can allow the therapeutic process to reach its maximum potential, through the therapist being fully relaxed that they are in a safe environment, and able to translate this confidence to the young person. However, whatever environment you choose, approaching this field of work in this way, can allow a carefully considered plan of approach to be achieved without the immediacy of pressure of being with the young person. Another example is a park location, and evaluating, whether there are peers around that might know the young person, and whether this is helpful or unhelpful for the session.

Developing an awareness of the weather conditions ahead can also be helpful, alongside checking forecasts, and thinking about appropriate clothing. I found that consulting closely with the family or foster carers of the young person, about appropriate clothing, if the weather is wet, or very hot is also helpful. Also, if the young person is going to get wet from an outdoor experience, such as from going along the sea shore, or in the safe part of a river, taking appropriate footwear, can save difficulties afterwards. A straightforward example was when, in one of my sessions, a pair of wellington boots could have saved wet socks and shoes, on one occasion! Taking waterproofs can also be helpful, and a woolly hat, or gloves if the weather conditions are cold, can allow a young person to feel much more comfortable.

Awareness of how cold conditions can affect someone is also important, through a change of their responsiveness or behaviour, e.g. gradual increase in irritability and how introducing warm clothing, that the therapist, or young person has brought, if on a mountain can quickly make a difference to them. Also, a quick departure from an exposed location, with high winds can be necessary. An early recognition of the above signs of exposure can be helpful too. If you have an outdoor qualification, and are running therapeutic sessions for a young person, in a specific location for a regular period, you will need to complete a risk assessment too.

Equally if conditions are very hot, taking plenty of cool water, and resting in shady places can make a difference, alongside a strong sun cream, and a sun hat.

Also, checking the tide along a beach, and having a tide table, can allow the therapist to know if the tide is incoming or outgoing, which can help when exploring around a headland, or near cliffs, to maintain safety.

Also, to ensure when travelling that your car is well prepared with petrol, oil, water, and is in a generally good condition, is important alongside adequate tyre pressures, and tyre tread. This can avoid anxiety for a young person who has enough issues without presenting concerns from the session. It is also important to ensure that you are covered with business insurance, which covers travelling with clients in a work situation.

If like myself you are working with animals extra preparations are essential including water for the dog, any food or treats which need to be given, often by the young person, a dog lead, if needing to walk through a busy area, and a ball and ball thrower, all of which need to be checked if they are present in the back of the car before you go. The young person often needs re-assurance that his new friend is quite happy and safe! It may also help to check with the young persons carers, if the young person is allergic to animal hairs too.

The Sea Landscapes

Introduction

The following sea environments were with young people, with whom I worked directly (one to one), of differing ages, who expressed different styles of communication, ranging from the symbolic or non-verbal to a verbal dialogue. The sea provided a rich variety of landscape ranging from turbulent coastlines to sheltered coves, rock pools to explore, or long sandy beaches with plenty of space. This allowed them to express creatively the affects of the physical, emotional, and sexual abuse, on their lives, and seek a way forward, with a sense of their therapeutic journey emerging. However, it is important, as mentioned above, to research suitable sea environments before the therapeutic sessions begin with the young person, and always be sensitive and aware of prevailing weather and sea conditions.

Many therapists use sand trays, pebbles, and shells, when working with young people and therefore the varied seashore environments can also be seen as life size expressions of this, or an alternative way of working, which may appeal to their clients. This section has two parts. The first part focuses on specific sea environments, which were used to help children in different ways emotionally. For example, a wide sandy beach allowed one young person to release tensions and anxieties in his life, by running spontaneously across the sands, allowing him then to feel able to talk about his issues. The second part involves a case study of a young person called Philip, who I worked with for a longer term period, in which the sea environment helped him to address issues of loss and abuse in his life.

PART ONE

USING ROCK POOLS

Rock pools are rich areas of marine life where interactions of movement, of different animals in a sheltered and protective area, can stimulate the young person to consider issues of safety for them from the power of the strong incoming tide, or other dangers. This can be empowering.

Therefore exploring the seashore rock pools of a beach can be rewarding therapeutically, and when identifying smaller animals such as a beadlet anemone, shore crab, or tortoiseshell limpet, can allow the young person to relate a strong incoming tide as powerful dangers to these animals, which need protection, just as their mothers, for example needed protection from a violent partner. There is the opportunity for the young person to apply with the therapist or support worker, ways to facilitate protection of the animals with a bucket and spade, for example, in which they can dig a hole in sand near the animals or rock pool, to allow a sense of the animal being further underneath and safer from the powerful sea. This I have found has given a real sense of empowerment, to the young person, that he is making a difference to the animals welfare without the need for verbal dialogue about the abuse he may have witnessed or experienced, and that he has made a difference to a dangerous situation, symbolically.

This may be helpful particularly if the young person finds it too painful to engage verbally about their past experiences, or has learning difficulties, or is of a younger age. Alongside the therapy, it is important to place guidelines for the young person explaining that the animals too need a lot of respect and care, particularly if this way of showing care is alien to what the young person has experienced in their family life.

Sometimes if the young person has shown a concern for some of the rock pool animals, or sea shore life, it can be frustrating in terms of ongoing processing for them, if in a following session with their therapist or support worker, there is a high tide which prevents them from going near the homes, or the same seashore environment of the animals they previously observed. They may feel a barrier against what they wish to do, or something out of their control just as protecting their mother, for example, from a violent partner, may have seemed out of their control as a young child. Therefore, a creative role-play or dialogue can be very helpful in engaging a younger aged child, in which the young person can play the part of a rescuer, or someone who can make a difference to the care of one of the sea shore animals, and the therapist can play the part of one of the sea shore animals.

When I have applied this through 'enactments', which may also include very rough or stormy weather conditions, it has allowed the young person to feel they are making a difference even if not on the sea-shore. This has included, for example, a young person, after being unable to get to the sea-shore, -because of a high tide-, suggesting we 'contact the animals (in role)'. The animal's names (e.g. Limpey) were all chosen by the young person, and matched by him to the type of animal or the species, after seeing them in a previous session on the seashore. The key characters were a limpet, whom he called Limpey, a shore crab whom he called Crabby, and a Beadlet anemone whom he called simply Anemone. I was asked by the young person to play the role of the limpet, and to contact him as a rescuer (in role).'

The young person was then telephoned (in this 'role play' he was acting as a member of the emergency services) by 'Limpey' (myself), saying that he was in danger and needed some help from another sea animal hurting him, and tough waves coming in, who responded (the young person) 'that we were on our way', and also told the aggressive sea animal 'to stop and leave Limpey alone'. The therapist can role play either one part (Limpey) who can now say that 'the angry animal has gone away', or simply 'things are better now', which can have a very empowering affect on the young person, allowing them to make explicit their feelings and desires when they previously have never been able to express them before.

LESSENING OF THEIR SENSE OF RESPONSIBILITY

Alternatively, I have also played a second part (changing voice tone) of an 'aggressive animal (this has included a crab and lobster), who has heard from the young person, and wishes to change, or stop. At the end of the dialogue, the young person was thanked, by Limpey, and this particularly had a positive affect. There can also be an ongoing thematic sense to this approach too, in which subsequent dialogues, or role-plays in further sessions, can involve 'script changes'. This reflects the different outlook of the young person from different stages of their therapeutic support.

In the above example, in a later session, the young person said to 'Limpey' or Anemone (the injured parties), that they will call the rescue services, or coastguard, leaving the therapist to play the dual role of 'injured animal and rescuer' (changes of tone). The key aspect is that the young person is able to allow someone else to take the main responsibility for the rescue or helping the injured animal, rather than needing understandably to 'be the rescuer' himself. I have applied this in my sessions, at the initiative of the young person, and have found that this has naturally been applied by them (after a period of time), reflecting a change in their 'ownership' of the situation, allowing themselves to let go of responsibility into the hands of 'experts', which can then lead to trusting adults more, in the course of time.

This theme can often be elaborated with other relevant animals coming into the dialogue (role-played by the therapist, but scripted or directed by the young person), representing other people who have affected the young person both positively and negatively, or those close to them. I have found this has included, a 'crab' being asked to build an underwater house by the young person for 'Limpey (the animal in need) and that it needed to be very high, and that crab's mother had asked the young person for help when the crab was naughty. The crab was then given a warning by the young person that he could go to prison if he did this again. This could represent an actual situation in the young person's life that he could safely express in the context of a dialogue or role play. This impacted 'Crabby' (in role) who changed! The theme finished with thanks for the young person by all the animals in the role play, which was very important to him rather than criticism, which he may have experienced in his early life with his birth family.

It is helpful if the child has seen all the animals on the sea-shore before the role-plays. This is an important ingredient, adding reality, which then allows them to step, even if not aware, into the very traumatic background which they have come from, but in a very safe way for them

THE SHORELINE

Some of the animals could represent or symbolise actual people to the young person who have abused him or abused a member of his family. This may also lead to strong anger which can be released in a positive context by the throwing of larger pebbles into the sea which can bounce onto the crest of the wave, which allow the young person to give expression to their feelings, and which can prevent them from demonstrating their anger onto someone else whether in the home or at school.

I also feel it is helpful for the therapist to stand alongside the young person to allow them to feel safe, in their expression of angry feelings which they may find frightening to show outwardly, and which otherwise could lead to them building up 'pent-up' anger within themselves. The therapist may also need to be flexible and could be asked by the young person to join them in this expression of anger, which can allow the client to feel that their feelings are understood and empathised in a deeper way by their therapist, which could facilitate further their emotional restoration. This could come in the form of helping them to pick up the pebbles, or in throwing the pebbles onto the waves with them. The key aspect is the sense of empowerment which they feel, and that they are not helpless in expressing their feelings, in front of someone else. Also, having the same number of pebbles as the child can be very important for them.

The awareness of the therapist can also be important to show the child 'larger waves coming in' (in safe weather conditions), which could get him wet, and which he has time to react to by stepping backwards, and which the child himself or herself, can also see coming. This can be releasing where they may have suffered violence or sexual abuse from a more powerful person, and not been able to escape from or have had advance warning of danger.

It may also be helpful to find an open and safe beach, easily accessible to the public, but also which has a sense of privacy for the young person too. I have found it helpful to research suitable beaches before a session with the young person, and during an introductory meeting with a social worker it can prove helpful to see if the young person is interested in this type of environment for therapeutic work.

The sense of boundaries being tested is also a key area where adoptive parents or foster carers can feel very challenged by the young people in their care, and where the young person needs to begin to understand his own self, and the people whose care he is under, by testing these boundaries, particularly, as mentioned above, if the expectation of behaviour is very different from what they have experienced in their earlier life with their birth family, or may have wished for.

UNDERSTANDING BOUNDARIES: THE SEA EDGE

The sea or tidal edge can be very helpful to young people who are unsure of what has been right or wrong from their own backgrounds, and moving up to the edge of the sea, before a wave comes and then stepping back, allows them to formulate an early sense of the importance of their own boundaries; that it makes sense to move back because otherwise they will get wet! This may be at a subconscious level, but they can begin to see that their own self-rule 'makes sense', and then begin step by step to see other self rules are necessary for their welfare, and therefore in the course of time, rules made on their behalf by those who care may after all be helpful to trust and follow.

Initially, however, it is very tempting to go beyond the sea edge for the child, and it is a supportive and aware therapist who can recognise that the young person needs space and time to explore what his safety area is. Therefore he/she may feel that they need to go beyond the tide edge, and if wearing wellington boots may feel a need to go up to the top edge of the boots, seeking even to test the therapist, as to how far they can go, and wondering if there will be a call to them to stop, even if they don't respond immediately. Therefore as well as giving the young person space, the need for a safe boundary may also be what is required. However, if they are allowed-within safe parameters to go the 'extra mile', it can also, be enormously beneficial for them to decide when they need to step back making their own decision, and fulfilling their own boundary. This may be testing for the therapist!

This can equally be applied in a low tide rock pool situation in which exploring where the animals live, allows the young person to avoid deeper pools and walk around them, which is a creative way of them making early boundary choices without realising it, too.

Often there is an initiative to take off their shoes and socks near the sea edge, and the therapist is asked to do the same! The sense of being together in this journey could deepen or quicken this process of recognising limits, with a challenge from the child being, to go as far as possible, before they make the decision to return. This is often resisted by them until absolutely essential, and may include some lower clothes getting wet, and jumping over waves to handle the situation. If the therapist is satisfied that the wider weather or tidal situation is safe, this can be valuable medium, often on wide long sandy beaches with adjoining rock pools, for the child to get his own early sense of the importance of boundaries and safety.

Developing a Sense of Identity: The Sand Castle

The formulation of a sense of identity can also begin to become a part of the traumatised child's awareness, I have realised, and this can be identified by processes in which the young adult builds higher sand mounds with an incoming tide, using a bucket and spade, often with turrets (the actual sand castle), and emphasises the patting down or firming up of the sand so that it becomes more resilient. The therapist, I feel needs to be very aware to join the young person if he is invited to do so (nearly always asked for) by his client, and this can lead to the young person standing on his sand mound, and looking assertively at the sea and beach around him.

This can be a landmark change in his personal development, and sharing this with other professionals at meetings, or with colleagues for their insights, at supervision can be valuable. This is often non-verbalised, and has a sensory and symbolic, sense for the young person, which they may not be aware of. The therapist can reflect on whether to intervene with an explanation (in the session), if he feels this is an appropriate time, or a contextual insight, 'you're feeling good about things', or to leave what is happening without any comment.

At the same time, the digging of ditches around the mound can also be very important, as the tide comes closer. The therapist may be asked by the child, to dig a moat around the castle, and for the child to see that he is directing something much more immense-the flow of the tide or sea into the ditch or moat can resonate powerfully, I feel, to what he could not protect or do anything about before. This is the violence, to either himself, or abuse to his or her mother, or another family member by someone more powerful. I have witnessed an emphatic sense of joy from a young person when seeing seawater being directed in this way.

Releasing Responsibility

The young person may also decide to stay on the mound while the sea is held back for as long as possible by the moat, and may wish to get shoes and socks wet, as they resist what seems to be happening (it may be worth mentioning beforehand to the child's parents, grandparents, or foster carers that this could happen). The therapist can weigh whether their sense is that the child can reach his own point of letting go-that within themselves they accept 'I cannot expect within myself to stand up to something much more powerful (the sea), and therefore I can jump back to the shore, at the last possible moment or whether he needs to intervene to support the child to step back before they get too wet or overwhelmed, and that 'it is ok to let go of things'.

This symbolically can also (as well as being empowering for the child) allow the fostering of therapeutic work to introduce to the child that they have chosen, with or without support, to let go of feeling responsible for their mound, which can symbolise the violence or abuse, which they had felt responsible for, and become less of a 'adult or parent child'.

This experience can lead as a stepping stone to understanding that there can be situations in life, like the sea coming around the mound, which they cannot prevent, leading to their own realisation that they could not have prevented the abuse which happened to their mother or father, or protected them. This can sometimes take a long process of time, as I reflect on one young person (aged under 10) whose biggest challenge was that he felt very bad about himself that he could not have protected his mother from what happened to her by another man, and that he needed to do something about this.

Sometimes while the young person is on the sand mound, he or she may ask the therapist, to build an escape ridge, to prevent their feet getting wet, while they may dig a large 'swirl hole' (the key aspect) within the sand mound, with their spade. This can be just before the sea breaches the moat and mound (like a Norman Mott and Bailey castle). This can often be preceded, by the therapist being asked to work hard to collect water from the incoming tide to fill the moat before the tide comes in or to pour into the swirl hole (so the child test things out), as it is being made, though the key aspect for the young person, is the building of the swirl hole, (which he or she stands by), and waiting for the tide to pour into the hole having breached the walls of the castle. They then have the opportunity to watch it disappear down the hole first, before jumping via the escape ridge to the shore (often only a metre or less away). There was a real focus by the child, I found, on the water going down the hole, before he or she moved away from the tide.

After this session, the child concerned spoke of the most special thing for him being seeing the water go down the swirl hole. A convener in 'supervision', spoke of this perhaps representing the emotions and all that the child had witnessed (violence to his mother), being released from within him, and going away, and it certainly I felt had a powerful 'releasing' sense for the child.

Another interpretative aspect may be that there is an immediate connection to the past traumatic event which the child witnessed (an overwhelming adult 'was' the overwhelming sea), but it is in a positive context-being with the therapist on the seashore and this time, he has made a difference, the sea has gone down the hole which he dug, and even though it is temporary he has nevertheless 'made an impact', or a difference.

Affirmation: Rock Corridors

The therapist can also be important from the child's perspective, as someone who affirms for him, that he really is making a difference, in what he is doing on the seashore. I was with a young person, who had suffered from witnessing violence to his mother, and neglect to himself, and was keen to find some stones to protect a beadlet anemone, and some limpets, in a narrow rock corridor of sea swell; this seemed to overwhelm them, from an outgoing tide. The young person very carefully placed some stones in the gap in the rock corridor in front of the animals; giving them good space, with the first stone supporting the second stone, and the second stone supporting the third stone. As he was placing the stones he suddenly looked at me, and said with precision, 'are you watching Martin'? I felt this symbolised a caring part of the child, who had not (in his eyes) been able to protect his mother, but he could protect these animals, and this seemed enormously important to him that I could see.

The sense of communication and the empowerment which comes from this, is crucial for the young person, particularly if what has happened to them (the abuse and neglect) is too immense to verbalise, or the anger so strong they cannot shape it, with another person, even a therapist or skilled support worker. The abuse whether sexual, physical, or emotional, which they had experienced in their earlier life, and/or neglect, can become too removed from what they see as acceptable in foster care or adoptive care, particularly if they feel a sense of shame for what happened. When they are safe in foster care, for example, with a very different social culture or even when living with other members of their family e.g. grandparents or special guardians, it can be very difficult to express what happened unless helped by another medium, such as the outdoor environment.

The Sands: Safe Communication for the Child

The use of wide-open flat sands can be enormously helpful too as a vehicle of communication, for the above situations, particularly if giving a sense of space, with freedom to draw images (e.g. with a bucket and spade). This often can come spontaneously, and be self-generating for the young person.

One example of this was a young person whom I worked with who drew a series of rectangular shapes, which he called spaceships, which were a short distance from each other. They had some curves associated with them, and a mother spaceship, shown by a larger rectangular or quadrilateral figure. It was important to him that there were no distractions around, though people in the near distance had no sense of restriction for him. He was then able to stand in the larger mother ship.

His situation, was where he had been taken by the police and social care from his parents for abuse and neglect to both himself, and his siblings, but which left him unable to easily accept what had happened, and recognising that he was very angry but unable to process why he was. He lived in different foster care placements to his brothers and sister, and everyone was split up in his birth family.

As he was standing in his ship he asked if I would join him and jump, rather than walk into one of the spaceships, which I did, along with my dog, who did the same. This immediately led to him, then joining the spaceships with a thin but strong line, so that everyone was connected, and we were able at his invitation to walk between spaceships, which he was pleased about, and meet up.

I was able to recognise that this symbolised to him the pain of the family being separate, and what he wished to do to redeem this situation, expressed through the thin line-though the spaceships were still separate. I asked him, if this was like his family being completely separate, and was this why he felt so angry, and he said it was.

This then allowed him to seek to understand, what it could feel like to be missed by others, in future sessions. He also began to verbalise how he felt, reflected in a subsequent session, in which he was attracted to a long thin waterway at low tide about one metre wide, with sea water still in it. He was keen for us both to jump this waterway, before observing a small inlet by it. This was a depression of sand, which he felt keen to dig with me, as a side channel, which slowly allowed the water to flow into it. It was more sheltered than the main mini channel, which seemed important to him, and which allowed him to suddenly say loudly that he was very, very angry with social services, for taking him away from his family.

This seemed releasing, and continued the gentle progress of his own connections of how he felt, and why. The key aspect was that this was a creative environment, which he felt safe in, along with a supportive therapeutic person. The sheltered inlet was symbolic of the safety of the therapeutic space for him, to increasingly share more painful things.

RELEASING STRESS AND ANXIETY

Wider space on sands can also give opportunity for the young person to be able to release energy and tensions from the day. This can be through running, for example, in creative ways such as in circles, of varying size, or in elliptical shapes, and in differing speeds, or by running from the beginning of the sands to the tide line with their therapist joining them, when appropriate. This can be in a linear or straight direction, and can allow stress and anxiety, to be released. I have worked with children who have used both circular and linear patterns on beaches, and have found them to be much more settled afterwards, and able to either talk or show symbolically, in a sensory way, their issues or concerns. A sense of immediacy of expression comes in this way.

One young person from whom I learnt the value of this form of expression, was just simply profoundly happy where he could run in directions he wanted to, in the safe confines of a wide sandy beach, and the therapist alongside, joining him! He had previously suffered many conflicts and uncertainties with adults concerning appropriate boundaries of behaviour, whether there were contradictions in standards from adults concerning their own behaviours, or in what they expected from him. He had suffered from sexual abuse from a family member he trusted, and also had to be taken from his mother, into care, with a number of foster placements, which had different social and behaviour expectations from his home life. He had also not been able to cope with standards of behaviour rightly expected in a mainstream school, and found special school hard to conform to.

Nevertheless, in the above situation, he could make his own choices-running in large elliptical and circular directions,-within strong natural boundaries such as the tide edge or dry sands, and the end of the beach, (alongside a supportive therapist), and slowing down or stopping when he was tired. He could also invite his therapist to be a part of his world, in which he can register through touch i.e. with the ground as he runs, his own sense of control and clarity. This is Proprioception, which is your body's ability to sense movement, action, and location, or know where it is in time and space.

There is of course, the need to intervene if you feel that the young person becomes unaware of his own tiredness or approaches a danger situation, but in the above situation, there was a gradual settling of emotions, with the young person both stopping at the right time, recognising the importance of his own boundary, and then being able to react to structures such as 'when to go'. In other words where the young person has come from worlds which have made no clear sense, there can possibly be natural mechanisms with skilled support, to allow him to see the value of his own guidelines and sense of care, and as said above this may be a stepping stone to allowing others – e.g. his foster or adoptive family – to introduce their care standards for him or her (i.e. he sees the point of it).

This could also be introduced verbally to him after this experience, to further support both the young person and his foster or adoptive family.

The young person also has the opportunity to create his own journey through making tracks on the sands. This can give him both a sense of empowerment of being able to get somewhere in his life, without restriction, (i.e. from point A to point B), and also an opportunity to reflect how hard or bewildering his life has been for him so far. This can be shown by a walking pattern on the sands, which appears not to go anywhere, or has a very gradual direction, which is both exacting and can go backwards, and then eventually lead where he needs to go.

This was also shown by the above young person, who made a very clear journey, which he wanted me to join him on, from one end of the beach to a half way point, with the outwards journey being expressed by walking upright, but the return journey (0.5 km altogether) being on all fours in which we both had our separate tracks, very closely alongside each other, and going in the same direction. It was very important to him to see that we made clear tracks, but which needed to include carrying quite large heavy pebbles, on the way back, which made the journey much more demanding. At certain points he would pass the pebbles to me to carry, until my load became heavier than his. There did not seem a controlling or angry sense, coming from him, but a more releasing sense, in which I was able to become the adult, and he could be 'the child', in terms of myself 'in role' playing the part named by the young person having more 'to contend with', or responsibility. We finished the journey with the young person feeling encouraged, as we both walked together on the short distance on the coast path back to the car, where he was very keen to keep the pebbles as a collection. There was a sense of clarity and progress in this experience, for him I felt, in 'how things should be'.

In another session, we made another sand journey (outward and return), which was initiated by the young person spontaneously, though this time it was much less clear, and involved a longer walk through the sands tracing the course of an out flowing river, in the middle of the sands. This beach was about 300 metres wide, and stretched for about 0.5km (at low tide). The journey was easier on the outward leg, as we followed the river, though it was important for the young person to allow my dog's ball thrower to float down the river alongside us, though he wanted it to be quickly rescued before we reached the more turbulent tide (his home situation was deteriorating at this time). This may have been his expression symbolically, at the same time the young person needs to be reassured that the actual sea animals have a natural protection from the rough sea by being within the rock pool without a need to move them of 'being' the thrower in the river, and an expression of his life or alternatively have been a straightforward fun focus. At the time he was living with his mother.

On the return journey, the testing of edges between sand and river water was significant for him, allowing him then to walk at a safe distance from the crumbling sand edge (this was a very low edge of about 20 cm). We both applied this, and again I felt this was his way of beginning to understand why boundaries, or rules in family life, can be important i.e. so that his shoes and socks do not get wet. Halfway back his approach changed, and he felt a marked journey line (with the dog thrower cutting into the sands) would be good, as we made our way back to the car, in which he would mark the route, asking me to follow exactly on the line.

This journey was not straightforward though and had many circles and loops, sometimes going backwards which made it very difficult to see progress towards the car. This seemed very important for the young person to express, with him inviting me during the middle part, to take a lead myself, and for him to follow me. He again took over later, and we made our way back to the start. I felt this symbolised how he felt about his life, perhaps in an unconscious sense (he was under 10) and whether somehow he felt he had to take the lead in his life, hence aggression when feeling that he is loosing that control (in his wider life) to adults who have roles of responsibility for him, such as foster carers or teachers, but it was difficult for him understandably to know the best route.

It was encouraging, that he allowed me to take the lead at some point, and interesting that following the contours of rocks were helpful to him at the end. This latter aspect could link to the safe boundaries and guidelines of a good foster placement.

Therefore, there is plenty of opportunity on a large area of flat sands, for children who have had very traumatised and abused lives to express their sense of confusion, or difficulty in understanding what has happened to them, and why, in a safe and releasing sense, without perhaps being conscious of this. Large flat sands therefore can allow an enormous sense of freedom of expression, within the guided boundaries of the therapist, for children to express how they really feel.

The therapist or support worker, may need to check the nature of the sands beforehand, and the state of the tide, as a high tide, can restrict this type of expression, though equally sudden short dashes or bursts towards waves at high tide and back as it comes in (if considered safe by the therapist) can also release tensions. This may be considered on a safe sandy beach, or slipway, and particularly on an incoming tide (non storm conditions).

THE STONY BEACH

The sea is also a powerful agent of change, as are streams, rivers, or estuaries, going into the sea, and the affects of pebbles being made smooth or like glass, can be sources of stimuli for traumatised young people, as can sands made very smooth by a strong incoming tide.

One young person I worked with spontaneously drew three circles in a very small space of sand, which he then said, was a happy face, a sad face, and an ok face, of himself, which can be accepted without comment, or followed up by the therapist. We then went on to explore the upper beach zone, where smaller pebbles were and discovered small skimming stones. The young person then suggested we have 5 each which we choose which are 'skimmers', and we both skimmed them to see 'how many times we could hit the sea with them'. This can both build the therapeutic relationship between the therapist and the young person, and also be a source of stimulus for the young person to feel confident to express himself, or that he can 'be himself' in sessions with the therapist.

In the case of the above young person it brought back memories of happy times with his 'Pap' and when they used to have fun and skim stones in the sea. The young person at this time was missing the closeness of being with other family members, while being under the care of his Nan.

Initiatives, by the therapist can also be taken, which can still be child-centred, when observing materials on the beach. I observed, for example, colourful smooth glass, and after bringing this to the young person's attention, he showed strong curiosity. I then explained how the erosive properties of the sea had smoothed the glass and changed it (using appropriate language for his age). This gave space for the young person to 'bring himself' into this 'arena' with him saying spontaneously, 'that's like my mum who is changing'. The young person is now able to see her, and was able to connect this imagery with painful experiences he had gone through with her in the past. This allowed him to express himself verbally, which was not possible for him in our previous sessions. This can also allow follow work by the therapist to continue this theme to help the young person (if they wish to), express more of this aspect of his life, with a view to understanding it more.

PART TWO

THE ROCKY COASTLINE: PROCESSING SHOCK AND TRAUMA: A CASE STUDY:

The sea environment can also be valuable for the child in care, who has been affected by a series of traumatic incidents in their life, and when looking for stability from the care system, finds that this is not easily working out either. The shock resulting from this can be supportively released where powerful natural forces are at work, alongside skilled therapeutic support.

One example, of this was Philip who was in care and was waiting to hear from the courts, whether he would be able to stay in his foster placement, rather than with his father. He had suffered severe physical and emotional abuse from him, and his mother had left him when he was a very young child. He wished to see his father on an occasional basis, but had felt happier in care and safer. However, the young person had been involved in a number of boundary issues with his foster carer, which resulted in him being told he would unfortunately have to leave his placement.

There was a sense of complete disbelief and shock as he spoke to me about what happened, identifying feelings of anger, sadness, and confusion. He had really liked this placement. He spoke for about half an hour.

I introduced Philip to a rocky and turbulent sea headland (we had been working together for about a year). We walked down a slipway near this point, where he paused looking at the sea in complete silence.

This took place for about 5 minutes where neither of us spoke. He was almost within himself or disassociating from the present, though at the same time the strong winds and sea were 'reaching' him, and he was engaged with this. There was a moderately strong sea swell (force 4-5), with the white sea-spray overwhelming nearby outlying rocks.

Philip then suddenly said, 'that this experience had really helped him and somehow he had let go of an awful lot'. He went on to say that it was like a release.

At this point we continued with a verbal engagement, and sensing that Philip may have felt he was at fault, I shared this with him. He responded that he did feel he was at fault, and while at the edge of the sea, reacted well when I asked whether he could begin to let himself off the hook.

He then focused on the birds on the larger outlying rocks (about 300 metres out to sea) saying that they were safe from humans, and yet they had no fear of the powerful waves crashing around them. This seemed a very valuable insight from him observing how well the natural world integrates, and may have in an unconscious, or conscious way brought a soothing sense, relating both to his sense of security, and overcoming his fear of his father.

Adjustments can also be hard for the young person to adapt to, if there are stricter boundaries in a placement, which come into being, or a sense of change from what he or she has been used to. These may be very necessary and right, but can leave the young person feeling confused if there is no dialogue concerning why they have been introduced, in a co-operative sense. If the boundaries are then broken, a consequence is understandable to present from foster carers or guardians, for the young person. This is a necessary intervention for the young person's own well being.

However, if the effort of the young person to adapt to the new rules or boundary changes, is not seen, at the same time as he makes a mistake resulting in a further punishment or consequence, then this can leave him feeling confused, angry, and disenchanted in his life. He may have witnessed this in his earlier life too, and therefore this could re-enforce his sense of being let down.

Further visits to a sea environment can help release tensions and anxiety for a young person, who is experiencing such changes of life style. This may link with something 'beyond and more immense (the sea) which is impartial to them, and yet he or she is a part of this, and can be themselves'. This can have an impact when issues of trust and truth arise, in which they may feel judged.

To avoid the consequence of not meeting a rule or boundary correctly the young person may seek to not tell the truth, causing further conflict, and this can lead to an unhealthy feeling about themselves, which they wish to change. However, this is very difficult, as it becomes a useful survival mechanism, which children in care may have needed to survive in their past life. Often this can arise if the young person feels 'cornered' by a situation.

Philip, in a subsequent session, spoke of bringing back his best clothes (to his foster carers), to change them, so that they would not get any mud on them, though he felt distressed that this was not recognised, and instead the negative aspect of him being late was picked up on. This made him feel angry, though somehow he was able to control his anger, he added, and show restraint, which felt strange for him, from how he had been in his past.

I was aware how Philip's self-image was affected by not being able to tell the truth, and I suggested, had he considered, 'telling the truth'. He responded that this was also seen as an excuse to get out of things. This could be his way of avoiding this challenge, though also it may be helpful for carers to support the young person for telling the truth, if this is perceived to be the case. I also suggested that he could simply say, 'yes I was late. I don't know why I did this', as a further step to move towards telling the truth'.

Philip did have to leave his placement, though he remains good friends with them. In a subsequent session, he spoke of his shock at what happened, and how unnecessary he felt introducing excessive rules were. He felt this served to create more tension rather than lessen tension, which could have been achieved through a more co-operative approach. This was a traumatic experience for him, and the key aspect, he added, which affected him was the suddenness of leaving, and having no time to prepare himself for this. There was a suddenness to his mother leaving too when he was very young, which could have amplified his distress.

He asked to return to the same sea headland that we visited before (i.e. consistency and familiarity), and spoke of the 'peace' of the rocky outcrops in a rough sea, and seeing a difference with the tide out, and that he liked the wind, which was able to help him to let go of things. Philip also went on to say, that somehow he could begin to make sense of things and hold back from blowing up, and that it made a difference by the sea. I felt that there was a strong and positive therapeutic affect taking place in a sensory way for him, and that seeing, feeling, and smelling the turbulence of the sea, by a rocky headland, was allowing him to identify, and release his inner pain, in a restorative way.

I asked Philip after this experience, what he most desired for the future, and he said, a flexible approach (in care) where he could be himself with some rules. Through the above sensory approach, I felt he was then able to both rationalise and make explicit his own desires, in a balanced way. His whole being, as a person was involved rather just his mind.

THE SANDY BEACH

We continued to visit the sea environment, varying things with a visit to a flat sandy beach (his choice), in which Philip noticed that he liked the waves coming in and that the pattern of the tide was different as it ran outwards, showed by the black lines in the sands. This could possibly symbolise, unconsciously for him, the variance he felt and contrast between the happy and the unhappy, or the good and not good dimensions of his care experience so far, or simply that 'things can change'. Philip was able to reach deeper levels of expression, on the beach, sharing 'that he really liked his old foster carers, and they were kind, and that he felt gutted and it would have been better to have worked things through'.

This was followed by a period of silence, as we both stared out to sea. He went on to say, as we walked away from the beach, of being able to understand things more now (for himself) as he actually spoke, and that he could let go, which was 'helpful'. He then expressed that perhaps there was a point, to his former foster carers' view that they could all remain friends, rather than have things deteriorate further, and that he liked his new foster carers. This conveyed that he could see other view points now, even if he didn't agree.

I can fully appreciate that other avenues or contexts of therapy can be used e.g. indoors through craft, but believe that the environmental landscape, has a valid part to play, in therapeutic expressions.

The Sheltered Cove

This theme of his life in care continued, when we visited a more sheltered cove, rather than large rocky outcrops. Whilst there he spoke about testing a couple of boundaries in his new foster placement, just to see 'their response'.

I asked Philip, how he felt at this time, and he said, 'weird, sad and happy', adding that he was with different people now, and felt under less pressure with rules, though missed the people he really knew. I affirmed that change can be positive, though didn't wish to loose the sense of attachment, which he had for his former carers. I asked him, how he felt now about having to leave his previous carers. He responded that he couldn't understand why he had to leave, or not so quickly, and it could have been worked through, as they did a lot to try and help him.

It seemed valuable to him to express his sense of confusion, as he looked down on the calm sea within the cove. His focus was towards the water, while we stood on a safe slipway. The therapeutic setting I felt was essential for Philip to feel at ease and confident to express deeper pain, and it was interesting that it was on a higher elevation to the sea rather than looking out at the same level as the tide. As he spoke, the visual image he conveyed on his face was total disbelief, with an almost nomadic sense. His underlying conveyance, was of someone completely lost, without a belonging, and having experienced this with his mother leaving from an early age, and father more recently not wishing to contact him, this recent upheaval in care, must have compounded his disbelief. Philip was able to express that it was a shock.

There was occasional 'eye to eye' contact in the therapeutic engagement, as we both looked out to sea, while he expressed his feelings safely. There were no people nearby, and the expression came very naturally. The therapist or support worker may need to gauge intuitively, the level of quietness, which is appropriate, though the real guide is the young person. In the case of Philip, it was 'no walking today but lets go by the sea'.

I asked how it felt actually leaving the foster home, and he said, his foster carer said goodbye and that was it. However, he went on to speak of talking with her since, and that they were going to keep in touch. This was a strong positive response from him, which could have resonated into the loss he felt as a young child with his mother leaving, but the difference now was that he and his foster carer both wished to keep in touch, and talk. Therefore the more positive context of this traumatic experience may have allowed him to reach the pain of what he couldn't express with his mother, for many years, and begin to rebuild from this. Also, our own therapeutic sessions, facilitated more of a sense of immediacy for him, in sharing how he was affected, allowing him to self-reflect and make explicit, how he was feeling within himself.

Philip was also fascinated by the waves, and observed them for quite long periods of silence, noticing (verbally expressing) that even in a calm sea that they can reach the cove powerfully i.e. in a settled care situation powerful emotions can still arise. I asked him, how being by the sea affected him, and he said, it was a peaceful feeling which allowed him to escape from things for a while. He seemed in no hurry to leave this situation, though we went to a slightly higher point, to get an over view of the bay. There were two strong waves coming in which captivated him, alongside observing sea thrift, hanging with just a small amount of earth to the cliff, which also struck him. I felt he may also be gaining an inner strength from these experiences too, and that possibly the thrift may have represented in an unconscious sense where he felt his own life was, and that a small amount of support (earth) can make a difference.

As his focus looking out to sea was at a deeper level, I introduced to him that perhaps we all like our lives to stay the same, but in fact they are in a process of constant change, and that perhaps the sea water coming in looks never changing, but in reality it is constantly changing the landscape, and that crashing waves may help us to see that things can never stay the same. The young person related well to this.

Following up visits to an outdoor environment can also be vital, and the journey back in a car can facilitate further processing, for the young person within the context of eye contact straight ahead, without the therapist and young person looking face to face. This can create a sense of a shared experience, but somehow the therapist is therapeutically 'with' or 'alongside' the young person more I feel, than if he/she is looking across to him.

In the above situation the sea environment seemed to create a receptivity, and strength, within Philip, and whilst in dialogue with him (on the way back to his home) I suggested that we can also, alongside strong support, look to our own understanding and strength within ourselves to find who we are, as well as those around us. We related this into the testing of boundaries whilst in care situations, and why we need to test boundaries, and that for some people it may be that they need to see if the person will stay with them, and not reject them i.e. Am I still acceptable and ok?.

Philip identified with this, and said that he had tested his new carers with two things just to see their response, and it was significant to him that they said that was fine, just learn from it. He was also perhaps wanting to evaluate how they would react to a break down in agreement or acceptable conduct, and whether another traumatic experience could be involved again, which for many young people happened in their birth families. He went on to say 'that when we (himself) test boundaries we have the curiosity of the young child and it's natural that we need people who will be supportive of us'. I felt this was a valuable insight and expression of someone who had suffered for long periods of his life.

I affirmed how important what he said was, and that 'thinking back to his early life, that there is nothing wrong with him, but it's the people around him who have their issues'. He seemed quite moved hearing this, as if it was a completely new concept to him. In other words if he can gain a sense of acceptability for himself, there may not be such an overwhelming need to test boundaries in care, where he may be seeking acceptability, or approval, having been abused or criticised before in his life.

HARBOUR SLIPWAYS

Often the natural environment, and in the case of Philip, the sea environment, alongside a skilled facilitator or therapist, can provide a sufficiently nurturing environment, for the expression of detailed verbal dialogue to take place relating to very painful or difficult issues. This seemed to happen when the main eye contact, as mentioned above, is parallel to the young person, and looking to the place of stimulus, in this case the turbulent sea; this was from the edge of a slipway, where our feet were almost touching the sea. There can then be some direct eye contact, which can vary according to the person concerned, and therapist's discretion, within this outward focus. I felt this had the effect of allowing Philip to talk to his own inner self, or deeper painful area, and express it to the therapist, as if he (the young person) was there at the time, but that this was only a part of the bigger picture of 'understanding'. The sea gave tangible neutrality for Philip, or a restorative ingredient, to begin to process things.

Philip (aged over 15) now felt able to speak about his most painful issue. He spoke of being very bothered, because his mother left him at an early age (he hadn't seen her since), and he didn't know why she left. This happened as soon as we reached the sea edge and paused. I wanted to understand how much he had known about his mother, and asked him, if she had been physically hurt, and he said, she was.

I asked, if it was by his father, and he said, 'it was'. I then went on to ask, if he had any feelings he could recall from that time, and he said, 'feeling very puzzled'. I suggested whether his mother may have, had to have left for her safety, and that it may not have been connected with her love for him (the young person). Philip, still with eye contact towards the sea, responded that this may have been the case and he hadn't thought of it that way, but it 'was helping him by the waves to talk about things', and he was beginning to understand more about his mother from talking. I clarified this (with immediacy), and asked, do you mean as we are talking now, and he replied, 'yes'.

On the way back from the slipway he went on to say, 'that there were some parts which he understood now and other parts which he didn't'.

Wild Beaches

This theme related to his earlier life continued in our next session, when we visited a different sea area, with a medium length sandy beach with dunes. I asked him 'how things were since we last spoke about his mum', and he responded that 'he still didn't understand everything and he wanted to know from her why she left (when he was aged 3), and what happened to her in her life since she left'. This was because the sense of suddenly hearing from her (through his Social Worker), felt 'overwhelming', he added. We continued with a natural pause of silence after this, where Philip enjoyed walking towards the tide line and throwing the ball for Lionel (my Labrador) across the shore.

There was a sense of there being enough space and background stimulus (quiet methodical and regular waves hitting the shore) from the beach area, to facilitate deeper expression, and I then asked him about his father. He shared that he hadn't heard from his father for a while, which made him feel sad that he wasn't concerned about 'his own'.

I felt therapeutically that this was a helpful environment for further dialogue, at a deeper level, and asked him, if things had always been difficult. He went on to say that he met his father for the first time (in terms of his childhood memory) when he was aged 7, when staying with his Nan, and that he felt he was 'cool', and he then went to live with his father. However, things began to change and he would get cross and shout and hit him, though not with punches but with his hand. This 'hurt', he added, and that he "felt upset, angry, anxious, and confused by all of this". This was the most spontaneous and natural expression so far, which came without any pause between words, and seemed to release his real self.

We continued along the beach head with dunes in the background, with Philip explaining more detail of his life: 'I went back to my room after and just sat there alone and that it felt lonely with no one to be there to help me, as my mother had left and my father's new partner supported him not me'. I empathised and asked him how he moved forwards from this, and he said, somehow he pulled out of it.

Philip wished to say to his father, 'why did you have to do this', and at the end of the session spoke of 'being able to let go of things through talking'.

In the next session, he asked to return to the same beach, but look down at it, this time. He said, that he felt clearer now why his mother left though still had some elements of confusion, and that he heard from her by letter and that she answered his questions as to why she left, 'that it was because of physical abuse by his father. He understood this, and also learnt from her that she had sent letters to him, after she left, but when she sent them via his Nan she sent them back. He hadn't realised this, he said.

He went on to say, 'I feel resentful to my Nan and happier that my mum did care for me, and resentful to my father who behaved badly to my mum and myself'. There was a deeper conveyance as we looked down at the sea, from Philip, as he said, 'I wished my mother and father hadn't argued and that my family could all have stayed together without this happening'. I reflected that there was a real sense of loss being shown.

This young person felt able to process further his loss, saying that he 'accepted that his mother had to leave for her safety, but was also left feeling why couldn't you have taken me with you?' He added 'don't I matter? '. At the end of this session, he shared that he felt better and understood his feelings more now.

Returning to a Familiar Seascape

There seemed a continuous process taking place each session now, as we returned to the rocky headland with a slipway nearby. Philip spoke of 'feeling relaxed by the sea and that it was helping him to release things'. There were moments of silence I felt, which seemed valuable to him, at a deeper level. He went on to speak that it changed things a lot knowing that his mother had to leave when she did and that she did care, and impacted how he felt about himself, that he did matter and was valued. He felt now it would be good to keep in touch with her, possibly by letter at first, and that he wished his dad could sort his life out and they could meet on occasions. There was a growing sense of emotional strength taking place with him, in which the sea environment alongside a supportive facilitator proved a positive experience for Philip to move forward in his life. He then began to speak much more about his commitment to his own life and his GCSE's at school, and new foster placement, and his ambitions for the future.

In conclusion, if the young person is happy to be in a sea environment in therapeutic sessions, there is a lot of opportunity and scope to facilitate a restorative process, from the traumatic experiences of their past. This took place with Philip who was both able to understand his feelings, and express what happened to him through identifying with the dynamics of the sea environment, allowing him to recognise that he was not at fault, and that his mother had loved him after all. This gave him the emotional energy to believe in himself, and move forwards in his life. The key aspect he identified was that being by the sea allowed him to talk to his inner self, as well as the therapist, and reach the most painful and repressed areas of his life. Through this with follow up dialogue, in which he recognised that his feelings and thoughts about what happened, actually mattered, he was able to piece together an understanding of his own identity. This has allowed him to believe more in himself and generate his own ambitions for his life.

Examples of how the Sea-shore can be used:

Environment
Rock Pools (animals).
Waves.
Shoreline.
Sandy beach.

Pebble beach.
Rocky peninsula.
Wild Sandy beaches.
Sheltered Coves.
Harbours/slipways.

Themes:
Care for others.
Releasing Anger.
Boundaries.
Releasing Stress
Self-discovery.
Empowerment.

Building relationship.
Traumatic situations.
Deeper self-expression.
Shock and disbelief.
Security and Identity.

SECTION TWO:

THE PARK LANDSCAPE

INTRODUCTION

The Park can be a valuable medium too, for therapeutic work in which the young person can have a sense of normality, and variety of expression. They can vary between small focused parks with a variety of play apparatus (e.g. swings, slides, and merry go rounds), medium parks with a fitness trail and apparatus, larger parks with a wilder nature and open field, sand parks with play apparatus, and skate parks. In most of these situations, there will be other children and adults present, which can often facilitate the client feeling relaxed with his or her therapist, or on other occasions they can be very quiet.

It is up to the therapist to research the park beforehand, to get a sense of the atmosphere of the park, and how comfortable they feel too in this environment, as well as the young person. There can also be a fluid dynamic to this environment, in which the park may be quiet with a happy atmosphere, and then change suddenly with a different group of people arriving. The therapist will need to be sensitive to this, and if appropriate intervene to move with the young person, away from this environment, although on most occasions, with previous research, this is less likely. The other factor involved is the nature of the young person's expression of abuse or neglect, and whether this is appropriate for the dynamics in the park, at the time. In the larger parks, I also introduced my Labrador, in our therapeutic sessions, when appropriate.

There follows two case studies of two young people whom I worked with therapeutically in this environment. The first case study, of Trevor related to the theme of significance, and the second case study, of Michael, related to the theme of nurturing.

CASE STUDY ONE: SIGNIFICANCE

INTRODUCTION

Trevor was aged 10, and placed in a long term foster placement, after suffering severe neglect with his birth family. He was very close to his two brothers and sister, and had found it very hard to come to terms with being, taken by Social Care, away from both his parents, and siblings. His siblings all lived in separate placements, and Trevor had felt responsible , with his sister, for his two brothers. Trevor had also suffered with his emotional development, and found it hard to relate with his peers, and keep up educationally at school with what was expected for his age.

He also had different expectations related to what was considered, by his school, to be appropriate ways of relating to people, and found boundaries hard to cope with. There also seemed a lack of awareness, it was felt by his school, and Social worker, of the feelings of other people. I was asked to see if I could help him express his real feelings about his traumatic background through therapeutic sessions in the outdoors which he was much more comfortable with. Because Trevor was functioning at a much younger age level he felt very happy choosing a park environment, for many of our sessions.

RESTORATION AND NURTURING (PART ONE)

Trevor very quickly asked to pursue a theme of enactments related to search and rescue in a local sand park. This involved falling off his boat (symbolically) in a very rough sea, and needing to be rescued by the lifeboat crew. My role was to symbolise the lifeboat crew, and I was on a life size wooden boat built in this local sand park. There was danger and turbulence in the rescue, in which I was tossed from side to side in the boat, while he was shouting for help, before I was able to throw a rescue line to him, and haul him up (in role). A conveyance of speed and danger were important aspects for Trevor as part of this dramatic role-play, in building reality, to our scene, alongside difficulty in him getting into the front of the boat in stormy seas.

When this was achieved, he conveyed a powerful sense of needing warmth from a blanket (symbolic) and immediate care from the crew, before going into the inner part of the open deck, in which he asked for a warm cup of tea, and some hot food. The above 'nurturing, or regression play' was 'enacted' by us, before he began (in role) to build up strength and confidence, in the lifeboat.

The significance of these enactments for Trevor may be hard to articulate, at the time, but it is interesting that one year later, with the support of some worksheets on relationships, which I prepared, Trevor was able to make his inner feelings explicit. He said, 'my mother and father didn't look after me, or my brothers and sisters, and they were allowed to watch the television all day, and then after tea we had to come down from our bedrooms, and watch what my parents were watching, and this could be a detective film or something like this, which wasn't suitable for our young age and should have been shown to us when we were much older. When I wanted a cuddle I was pushed away, and felt my parents didn't care for me, and when my younger brother was frightened, I went to comfort him with my older sister, in his bedroom, as he had seen something frightening my parents were watching.

We were like a mum and dad to him, and then we were sent up a dark street to get some food for my parents, when we were young, but our mum and dad did not give us proper food and we had to have pot noodles all the time, and my father hit me'.

The theme of nurturing in our sessions continued for about 3 months (we met weekly at that time), and also included requiring medical help, from an air ambulance and medical staff. In one session, ambulance and staff (role played by myself) needed to revive Trevor (this was applied symbolically by myself without touch contact but with appropriate arm movements indicating CPR), and when regaining consciousness he felt he had to decide whether to go to a surgery or hospital.

In another session, after being rescued by the lifeboat crew (on the same boat in the park), we introduced an air ambulance, after Trevor spoke of needing emergency help quickly and was lifted (in role) by a winch up to the air ambulance. It seemed very empowering for him to be able to express as part of the enactment, 'that his bones were broken and what was going to be done to care for him'. There was an importance, for him, of as much reality, in this enactment as possible being involved, with his elbow supported by himself, and with padding being used (in role) to support his lower leg.

These scenes, even if not matching actual reality, had a very incisive symbolic significance, for Trevor, to the neglect that he suffered in his early life, and felt very empowering and restoring for him. It may also have allowed him to touch his early life, in a very safe way for him, without engaging verbally about his or her abuse. This was through expressing in role-play (e.g. a need for a warm blanket and hot food and drink), what he felt should have been done to care for him by his birth family.

This could also give him his own sense of what he feels is right conduct, and how people should behave, through the active participation of the therapist, who may therefore have a longer term impact beyond the sessions, in terms of guiding the young person to his own evaluation of how to behave in the future, and through this the early signals towards forming his own sense of identity. The enactments become a joint partnership, or a tacit acknowledgement for the young person to demonstrate how he really feels.

This was further reflected by the introduction of my Labrador, called Lionel in one of our sessions. Trevor responded well to him, and suggested that we needed to provide water for him, as it was a hot sunny day. The sand park had an adjacent playing field, which was ideal for this. I supported this (there was water ready to use in my car), and Trevor showed real pleasure in pouring the water. He also enjoyed throwing the ball for him, and although he needed guidance when loosing patience when the ball was not returned immediately, he showed real affection for Lionel (not displayed before) and gave him two hugs. This experience allowed him to show both care and affection, which he felt were not shown to him in his earlier life.

In the case of this young person, two additional scenes were involved, in every rescue enactment.

(1) Managing Conflicting Emotions

Firstly, I was asked to be rescued by Trevor afterwards, following the same contexts of a rough sea, and under very difficult conditions being hauled into the lifeboat, and cared for, which I felt gave a sense of further empowerment for him. Secondly, he would need to put himself in further danger (after having been rescued!), either by, returning in a rough sea to his boat, where he was capsized and needed to be rescued again, and in another session, falling from his boat into a deep part of the sea and needing to be rescued by a diver (myself).

There was a sense coming from Trevor that, he was not going to make it easy to be rescued, which may link with his attachment to his own mother and father, and anger at being separated from them (he was in long term foster care while these sessions were undertaken), even though he suffered enormously and felt angry about how he was treated in his early life. There was therefore a conflict involved for him.

These enactments can also be releasing for the young person if anxious. In the case of Trevor, he was due to see his parents the next day after our session, for supervised contact, and was slightly more agitated (though excited too), and wished again to put himself into the dangerous sea to get to his boat. This time, he was concerned about an injection – he explained no further-, though felt the risk of swimming in the rough sea (after initial rescue) was achievable if I came with him. We both acted this out through swimming actions over the sand until we reached a swing tyre, which represented his small boat.

He then took an imaginary liquid sedative, which put him to sleep (his initiative) in the rough sea, while we returned to land in his boat, for further medical help. This role-play allowed him to release a lot of tensions, as one of his real concerns was whether his parents would actually come to see him, and this may have felt quite overwhelming to think about.

(II) Expressing Reality

Following this theme, Trevor's enactments changed direction from search and rescue (nurturing) to training and responsibility for others, which was also a key aspect of his early life. This was also a year before he made explicit what his early life involved. We were both in a different sand park, which included a large model steam engine with a passenger carriage. Trevor decided to be a train driver, and suggested I could be the passenger, though very quickly he added that he needed to train me, to help with the engine, and understand the different speeds it could go, and where I could look out of the steam engine. He then observed (in role) that there was a fault in the engine, and he would need to climb on top of the engine (this was only a very moderate height from the ground), to rectify what had gone wrong.

I decided to intervene (in role), and suggested that we could slow the speed of the engine down to make it safer or easier to mend the fault. However, Trevor seemed more at one with danger (in role) saying it was fine and to keep the same speed going, which matches the reality of the challenge and difficulty in his early life. However, at one point he began to slide off the engine, and at that point he invited me to rescue him, although he soon brought humour into this situation, sliding from side to side, on the engine. The session finished with Trevor being thanked by the station staff (myself in role) and passengers for mending the engine, and allowing it to get back to the station safely.

This appreciation, for his work, was significant for this young person, who seemed moved, and said this felt unusual as an experience. In his earlier life, the responsibility Trevor had taken on may have been taken for granted, and this role-play may have highlighted to him that what happened in his past life, differed with how he is treated now.

EMPOWERMENT (PART TWO)

From the above phase of nurturing play therapy, which Trevor desired, there was a movement forward to enactments, which allowed him to develop a confidence and self-belief in himself, about his life.

They were a symbolic reactivity, by Trevor, to his early life experiences, which were expressed through creative therapy in the environment. These more mysterious expressions were nevertheless a progression for Trevor, from the restorative role-plays above, which may have provided a basis of emotional strength and energy to undertake the next developmental stage of more pro-active processing i.e. empowerment.

On one occasion, I was with Trevor, in a larger water park, and asked to pick up a medium size stone (we both collected the stones beforehand) for each of four man-made tunnels adjacent to the park, which had some discharge water running through them. Trevor then asked if I could throw them, one at a time into each tunnel, which he said he had thought carefully about before. This needed to be done accurately, and he felt very pleased when this was achieved, but frustrated when one stone wasn't and hit the side of the tunnel. I had another go and succeeded. It was interesting that this was the first time Trevor felt able to allow me to 'take a lead', with a sense that this was too difficult for him to do.

We then proceeded to the water lake in the park, and with the rest of the stones we had collected, he asked me to place one stone into the water, at one corner of the rectangular lake at exactly the same time as he placed his stone at the opposite end. This was followed by a second stone midway along the width of the rectangle, which we both placed at the same time, and a third stone which I had to place in the other corner of the rectangular lake, at exactly the same time as he placed his at the opposite end. After this 'enactment', nothing was spoken, though he seemed strengthened and empowered.

Trevor then asked if we could take our shoes and socks off, after noticing a small stream which he felt we needed to walk through. Following this upstream through the park against the force of the water, symbolized for him he explained being like a fictional character on TV who was able to overcome adversity and time (he could go into the past or future). Trevor wished to identify with this character as he had very little control over events in his own life.

We then went one behind the other, into the stream, in an exact line, which seemed important to him. As we walked through the water, I had an emerging sense that for Trevor this represented being washed clean from events in his life which he may have felt to blame for, and that this releasing sense was reflected in his desire to stay in the stream water as long as possible. At this point a mother and child interrupted the 'therapeutic space', in a kind sense, and Trevor, was happy to collect some leaves for the ladies daughter from the stream.

This is an example where one of the challenges of environmental therapy can be an interruption beyond the choice of the young person or the therapist, from a member of the public, though Trevor seemed happy with the sense of normality which this conveyed, and also with being able to have fulfilled his 'deeper expression', relating to stones and water.

I felt that his expression needed to be kept very private within him, as this seemed to be a very releasing and restorative experience for him, enabling him to move forward in his life.

This young person then built up the confidence to be able to express himself further, in the two sand parks, which he was familiar with, and which were secure environments for him. He also intuitively found the resources within the sand parks, which could facilitate this.

Initially he focused on a sand bucket with a winch, in which I filled up the sand into the bucket, while he was on the next platform level above me, and when full, pulled up the bucket with the chain winch. Trevor was then able to lower the sand, down a chute and see it successfully released onto the ground again. There was a sense that working together as a team was invaluable to him, in whom we had a similar purpose, and also that he was understood. In his secondary school situation, he was functioning at a much younger learning and emotional age, and this was understandably, not understood by his peers. To seek to gain attention from them he sought to react like a much younger child, though this resulted in them laughing at him. He was keen to get approval, but realised this wasn't working for him.

This confusion was further reflected when he changed apparatus, to a slide, in which he wanted to slide down, but with a head first approach. He was kicking his legs, but found that could not move upwards or downwards, and was stuck. He had likened himself to Dr Who (in role), and refused support from myself (in role as one of his team), to help him get down the slide.

He had, as mentioned above, not received the care from his parents, which he had wished for, and had to be responsible for his younger siblings. This, 'freezing' behaviour continued for a few minutes, and his narrative was 'that cyber men were watching us whom we couldn't see', and that I needed to keep out of sight of them. This interpretation changed after a short period, when he felt that Amy Pond (Dr Who's colleague) had caused the problem of him being stuck, using an 'ant burrowing machine', and even though she was on his side, hadn't realised what she was doing.

It seemed, that Trevor was demonstrating that the affects of people seeking to help him were paralysing for him, although he was aware that no harm was meant. It was proving very difficult for him to be 'reached' by the authorities. He then after demonstrating his concern, slid down the slide very quickly.

After a short break he wished to continue with a further enactment, and changed apparatus to the same steam engine and its passenger carriage (this was a scaled wooden model large enough for children to play on in the sand park), we had previously utilised. Using a child centred approach can facilitate a real sense of empowerment for the young person, and an opportunity for him or her to demonstrate issues affecting them in their lives, either consciously or sub-consciously, in a safe way.

Trevor, wished to be an engine driver, called Dr Who, and I was to be one of his passengers (in role) situated in the carriage behind. He then in role stoked up the fire of the steam engine, before the engine suddenly (his narrative) came off the line and the passengers (myself) were thrown from side to side in the carriage, which I enacted. This may have symbolised the suddenness in which he was removed from his birth family, and siblings (who also went into care). I was urged to demonstrate this very dynamically by the young person e.g. "put more into this"!

UNDERSTANDING (PART THREE)

After this the engine driver (Trevor) went into the engine tunnel (in role), and disappeared in smoke and heat. The passengers (myself) were very worried and concerned, though the driver then returned to rescue the train and allow it to get back on the track. However, crucially for this young person, the identity of the driver was not revealed to the passengers, for a few minutes, and when he did choose to reveal his identity, as Dr Who (himself), there was a dramatic entrance display. The intuitive sense I had was that he was seeking an understanding that he could be missed, in a way, which could protect him, and therefore in processing this, the passengers (myself) jumped up and down with joy and amazement. Trevor was watching carefully, my reactions (in role). He reacted very well to this, and I felt that there was a deeper desire, within him to wonder whether he could be missed, as his own person, by people he felt safe to test this out with.

This may link with questions in his own mind as to whether his parents miss him, and how missing someone is shown, and also that he can begin to allow himself to recognise that he too can miss people. The question I was reflecting was whether a completely new emotional experience was being created, in a safe narrative or role-play, by him, to understand for his own life too, and whether this was the early beginnings of forming his own sense of identity. The eye contact from him was seeking an understanding, perhaps, of 'do I matter to others', and the enactment conveyed, 'yes you do'.

This theme continued for a period of 3 months. In a subsequent session, we went to a Skate Park. This focused on Dr Who (Trevor) being helped to the top of the skate ramp, by one of his team called Mickey (myself). He succeeded after two attempts, after which Dr Who suddenly disappeared. In this enactment, I dramatised, the team feeling distraught, with the Dr intervening to say to us, that he was looking for many different ways to return to us from the South Pole. I was sitting at the top of the ramp and the 'Dr' then attempted different ways to get up including running and holding onto my feet, and then running and holding onto one hand to pull him up, which didn't succeed, before suggesting that he runs quickly up the ramp to me and I pull him up with two hands. Following this he reached the top. There was a sense of desperation being conveyed by the Dr (Trevor) in these attempts, which I felt might symbolise his feelings about being separated from his parents or his brothers and sister, and his desire to be with them again. However, his uncertainty too, in which he may be wondering whether he is missed by his family, and therefore demonstrating these feelings, in role, may be very important to him.

The skate park was quiet with few other young people around and therefore the mood of the park, whether quiet or lively and dynamic, may be an important ingredient for children or young adults, to weigh up, before feeling safe enough to express themselves. Some young people may equally need a lively and dynamic atmosphere. This type of creative environment can also facilitate a transition for Trevor from hidden symbolic expression, concerning traumatic events from his or her past, to an opportunity to hear from the therapist a sense of their own 'inner voice', or what they cannot yet fully express.

Expression (Part Four)

This was reflected in a development to our role-play, in which the feelings of happiness by Dr Who's friends at his return were suddenly dashed when he responded 'that this was not him (Dr Who)'. He was looking for our reaction, and therefore we conveyed enormous pain and disappointment. This may have reflected, the young person needing to see again how he was regarded by others i.e. that he could be missed, but also how his hopes of seeing more of his parents or being with them again, were not materialising (they do have regular supervised contact for short periods of time, though his parents did not always arrive). Trevor may also have felt very let down in his life, by his family. At this point he suddenly said to his team (myself), 'that it really is me, the Dr'!

I decided to follow up the enactments with verbal dialogue, and for the first time, asked him 'if he was aware of how sad we were when he was away', which he didn't find easy to react to saying, 'I don't know', with an almost dismissive sense. I returned to this theme later in the session, and introduced to him, that when he was away in the South Pole, we were very sad, but the hardest time was when we thought he had returned, and then our happiness was dashed painfully. At this point Trevor nodded and seemed to understand more; more, that he was missed by people, and he did matter. This awareness that other people close to him could show their loss and grief when he was no longer present was very important for him. This would be particularly relevant if he was not sure if his birth parents really missed him, or they had not been able to convey to him their sense of loss, after he went into care.

This was reflected in a later session in the sand park, with a similar enactment to the above, in which the disappearing train driver, returned again to his passengers, as another driver, though suddenly it became Dr Who again (himself). The conveyance from him this time, was 'I will not abandon you', and 'it's really me'. The passengers again looked very pleased i.e. myself (in role), which allowed him to verbalise "we will all be staying together", which was a real development, in expression of feeling for him. In the reality of his life Trevor, who took most of the care responsibility with his older sister for his two younger brothers, before going into care himself, had found it harder than any of his siblings to let go of his sense of responsibility for them, but until now had not been able to express this, through enactment.

This led in a further session, with a similar enactment, to a question from me, 'that perhaps the Dr coming back to life was your way of wanting to understand that you could be missed, and that this was what you wanted to know about your family, whether they missed you'. He listened very carefully, without comment.

However, this led to him, inviting me in another session, based in the sand park, to take charge of the train while he went into the passenger carriage, before he needed to come back and repair the steam train. He was beginning to let go of his sense of responsibility, even though this was a difficult process for him.

However, this led to a dramatic change of focus for him in future sessions, in which he wanted to go into the sand park to find new friends from his school, for the first time. I supported this, from a sensitive distance, in which he was able to engage with them for a short time, and afterwards expressed "I have never had this happen before where I could be myself and play with friends".

Conclusion

In summary, the above environments provided the essential creative space for Trevor, with a child centred approach, to move from needing to be rescued, and receive nurture and care himself,-gaining the necessary emotional strength-, to then express how difficult it was to let go of his responsibility for his family. This then allowed him to express symbolically (through embodiment play) how much he wanted to return to them, and the grief and loss involved for him, and to explore what it really meant to be missed by others, and whether he mattered to his family. It led him to begin to develop a sense of who he was, his identity, alongside being able to trust adults more to take charge, and begin to feel that he could be himself more to seek out friends of his own age. This process could also only happen with a safe and very supportive therapeutic space and foster placement.

Case Study Two: Nurturing

This was important to another young person, Michael, in long term foster care, who had suffered from neglect from his mother, at an early age. He found it very hard in the past, to express and understand his feelings, which he found easier (at first) to show visually in our sessions, rather than verbally. The opportunity to visit a town park, with apparatus in, was appealing to this young person, and gave him a sense of something to look forward to. There was a conveyance that he could relax within himself, and this allowed him to share on the way to visiting the park, experiences which he found hard from his past life.

He recalled two key incidents when living with his mother. The first was when he was hit on the head, with a brick by his friend (living close by), expressing how angry he felt with his friend. He showed this by a grimacing face, 'I felt like this Martin', he said, and he made the sounds of anger, saying 'and I sounded like this'. He added, 'I knew that he didn't mean to do what he did'. I encouraged him that he expressed how he really felt, and also that he linked this with a reason-the brick falling on his head. He went on to say that he punched his friend in the face after this. I shared that it was ok to be angry, without at this early stage focusing on how to channel the anger -I was aware that the young person was feeling bad about what he had done-, and that both feelings, acceptance i.e. seeing it was not meant, and anger i.e. feeling very cross, although different, were understandable to have.

He then quickly went on to recall a second experience, in which he fell over and hurt his wrist: 'a big part of my wrist came away, and it was only held by a thin muscle, and I gave a loud shout', which he demonstrated to me, in facial expression, adding 'I was at my friends house. I was feeling very upset and cried'.

I felt that he was beginning, without realising it, to understand his feelings. He went on to say, that his mother was next door, and that he felt really pleased when she came, but also very angry with her that it seemed to take so long for her to come.

He then said, that he and his mum went to the hospital, and his mum left him after an hour, while he stayed at the hospital for a day. I empathised with him how hard this must have been and re-enforced that we all can have very different and conflicting feelings. The young person seemed to understand himself more after hearing this.

When we reached the park, which he had always wanted to go to, he went straight to the swing slide, which he found really good fun. It was interesting that he was looking around very cautiously to other children nearby, and very aware of them,

We went back to the same park in a subsequent session; Michael went quickly to climb on the apparatus, observing the other children playing on the apparatus too. He was looking to see if I was watching him, and when I affirmed some good moves on the apparatus, and how well he was doing he looked really pleased. He then, asked the children nearby if he could join them, and they agreed, and then had a lot of fun, and although there was a caution, he was clearly enjoying the experience (he knew one of the children from his school). There was a desire to keep engaging with them. I was able to position myself on a nearby seat, and he felt able to leave his drink with me, and then return when he was thirsty to get his drink, before returning naturally to play on the apparatus. He observed me watching him all the time, and then relaxed into a very natural flow of awareness, that I was there, and that he could also begin to 'be himself' and play with other children. At different moments of time though, he would still need to check that I was watching him.

While this was happening there was a short but significant moment of time, where he almost disassociated from the immediacy of his play, distracted by a young mother caring and supporting her young son (aged about 3) on a swing. She was gently pushing him backwards and forwards. He was fascinated by the interaction between them. Their eye contact also seemed very important to him, and he watched them closely, conveying that this had priority, over anything else. After a few minutes he returned naturally to play with his friends.

I felt this had a powerful impact on Michael, perhaps not only in recognising what he may have missed out on, in his early life, but on how things should be. In other words as well as reflecting his own sense of loss, he also was learning how interactions should be, which I have recognised in some of the above situations with other young people.

There is therefore an indicator that children may be recognising for themselves what they have missed out on, and also learning how things should be, i.e. with the mother and child's interaction on the swing. This happened again in a later session in which the young person became deeply focused on a father walking past our seat with his two young toddler sons, watching carefully in case they fell over, and then gently picking them up. There seemed a real sense of longing being conveyed by Michael while watching this interaction, as all other aspects within the park faded away for him.

The therapeutic space provided by an environment such as a park, can also allow the young person to release presenting tensions and anxieties affecting their life. Michael had been very worried about a song, which he found hard to perform as a solo, at a school concert, and was able to express that another girl was helped with group support and he wasn't. This he felt was unfair, and resonated with deeper pain concerning unfairness in his past life. Michael felt better expressing his feelings, which he could now do verbally rather than visually.

He then felt able to show his skills on a moving slide rope in the park, and developed different techniques, successfully, including a one handed approach at speed. He seemed very encouraged, and expressed feeling proud of himself. This was a very positive self –expression. Therefore there is opportunity to develop self-esteem in this type of environment.

I was aware that Michael was soon to meet his father for the first time in many years, and asked him how he felt about this. He felt able to express, immediately, that he felt nervous at first when thinking about it, and then happier and excited. This allowed him to continue to express further feelings, sharing that he was feeling happy with his new foster carers, and that past experiences in his foster placements had been more difficult for him.

We also visited an alternative town park, to vary activities, which included a Zip wire, and wire climbing pod. In this situation, Michael was very pleased for me to join him, and felt very happy being able to feel challenged on age appropriate resources. Therefore the therapist or support worker will need to have flexibility, and clarify with the young person what they feel comfortable doing (which may be all the activities), and what they do not, either before the session, or during it.

In a subsequent session, Michael asked to return to the park he was used to, having arranged to meet a few school friends whom he was comfortable with, during the time of our visit. There may be a need therefore for a more encompassing person centred approach to therapeutic sessions i.e. allowing others to join in the session. The therapist will need therefore to understand what is going on within the young person to feel able to invite friends. I felt there was a slowly growing change of thinking with this young person, recognising that most children may be ok now. There may then be either a need for an affirmation of this, or running with this silently, or a need to intervene to say this unfortunately is not appropriate, depending on the situation and young person.

I felt, in the above case, this was an important development for the young person's social confidence, but which also related to the sense of nurturing which has gradually been building up for him since identifying with this park, in our sessions. Michael and his school friends played football, asking for me to join them, and also played a chase game on the apparatus. He seemed very happy, and more confident in his interactions with them than before, with good eye contact between him and his peers, and a real sense of co-operative play. Afterwards he said, 'this was good fun'.

Michael also expressed on the way home, that being able to talk about his concerns about the school play had been most helpful to him so far, and when I asked him how it felt sharing about his two traumatic experiences when with his mother, responded that he felt relaxed and able to talk about this.

The journey from the park to Michael's home, is about 20-30 minutes in time, and was a valuable space for the young person to express himself. Allowing the child to have environmental experiences, which are relevant to them, such as being in a park, can facilitate deeper expression by them, and an openness to understand more. This can only be built up through trust, with the person whom they are working with.

On this same journey Michael spoke of feeling moved about a parable, which was spoken about in a lesson at school, which he shared with me. This focused, he explained, on the owner of a farmhouse who was evicted by the council and it became a dump. The elderly farmer, who was the owner, returned to the site of the farmhouse every day, and then after 10 years the farmer fell asleep one day, and a lady from the council said, 'you can have the land back now as a farm again, and all the animals returned with the farmer'. I asked Michael what impacted him most about the parable, and he said, it was the farmer returning to his land every day, and having his land back. He went on to say, 'that he felt very angry that the farmer had his land taken away from him'. He also said that he was affected by the animals returning with the farmer to stay on their land, and that they went back with the farmer each day during the ten years, but hid from the lorry drivers who went to the dump.

I felt that this was a valuable expression for Michael of the loss he suffered from his own birth family and particularly his mother, and very gently suggested this to him. It seemed very helpful to him to talk about his reactions to the parable, though very raw, as even the slight beeping of my car around a bend could lead him to say, 'stop beeping'.

I also felt the parable may have allowed him to recognise that he also would like to return to his mother one day, along with his brother who lived in another foster placement, reflected by the animals returning with the farmer. There was perhaps though a deeper sadness and grief he was seeing where, what the animals and the farmer were doing i.e. returning to their home, he could not do and that this was right, but a part of him wished that it wasn't. He often would seek the comfort of chocolate, which was a strong attraction for him, though talking about his deeper issues, through the parable, was an important aspect of progress for him.

In a subsequent session, when we were travelling to the park, he said 'I am most concerned about the school play, and that someone else was chosen instead of me to sing my song, when I had been practising it, and this boy did not have the voice that I had, and I've had enough taken away from my life as it is'. I felt this was an important expression of how he felt. He added that he felt angry and frustrated about this. There was a pattern emerging of a major sense of loss, linked to his anger, for Michael. He also suffered a repeated breakdown of foster placements, after leaving his mother, up to the present long term placement.

There was more fluency of expression now from him, concerning how he was affected by events in his life, and how he really felt. The underlying focus on the park gave a releasing and restorative sense to his loss, allowing him to engage verbally both before and after this therapeutic experience.

At the park he engaged with a similar group of children, though I observed a growing confidence in his interactions with them i.e. he was listening to what they said, and they were responding to him, though there was also a need for regular eye contact with myself. I was positioned on a seat a short distance away from the slides and climbing apparatus. I acknowledged this each time with a supportive nod, which was registered by him, observing throughout. There was a nurturing aspect of this play emerging increasingly, both through his interactions with myself i.e. looking to see if I was watching and showing interest in his chase game with his friends, and through his increased levels of conversation and negotiation with his friends i.e. asking who is chasing now, and where is safe ground from being caught. He also asked to stay with his friends slightly longer, which was encouraging.

There also seemed to be a conveyance that he was regaining an aspect of his life, either lost, or which he may not have experienced before, through interacting with new friends in the park, some of whom he knew at school. This seemed essential to his self-confidence. On other occasions with less of a group I was asked by him to engage in a chase game too, on the apparatus, which he really enjoyed, encouraging me to apply this more in our sessions! This may relate to the absence of his father, who he was going to see again, after a number of years' absence. Therefore it is an interesting question, whether the therapist plays a mentoring role in both a male and female sense, symbolising what the child would have needed from his mother and father, though in a dynamic sense needs 'in the present' too, as part of their restoration.

After this experience at the park, on the journey home Michael spoke of a strong desire within him to care for animals, and bring up a foal (he was aged 11) under his care. He added that he wasn't sure how to raise this with his foster family, and asked if I could. This may possibly be an internalised sense of nurturing taking place, which could be fulfilling a gap within him, and also a way forward for him in showing how animals should be treated. I had observed this behaviour in other children too who have suffered from neglect from their birth family. I did share his thoughts with his foster family, who were going to discuss this further with him.

On the same journey home, while having a break at Asda, he asked me, 'what I thought of him', and that he didn't mind bad things being said. I responded with positive affirmation since knowing him. I felt he was in a very open place of trust, therapeutically, with a desire to understand who he was, and how he could begin to believe in his own inner self. I spoke of his care and consideration for others, and his honesty, and felt (self-reflection) he was beginning to shape his own sense of identity, as reflected in his interest in caring for a foal. He later spoke of enjoying talking in between playing at the Park, and it was good saying how he felt about things.

In summary, Michael showed a growing self-confidence through experiencing the park environment both within himself and with his peers, in play, and through my affirmation of this he felt supported, and able to gradually explore further and widen the boundaries of expression. Alongside this he observed different social behaviour between very young children and their parents to what he had been used to which impacted him positively, and after these park experiences felt able to express deeper issues and presenting issues very openly and honestly, developing his communication from visual expression to verbal expression. This allowed him to understand why he felt so angry and that it was positive to express this. It also enabled him to begin to shape his own views of life, in a real sense rather than what he felt others would approve of him saying, and through this, to self-actualise, or begin the journey to find his own identity.

In Conclusion, to this section, the above therapeutic interactions in the park relating to Significance, and Nurturing, were a rich source of stimulus for the young person, allowing them with skilled support, to both understand and express deep and difficult issues in their lives, in a safe and secure way. They also reflected different approaches to working, one involving dramatic narratives or role-plays, and the other actual realities of interaction, with peers and families. The therapist can facilitate this process, allowing the young person to both understand the affects of their past life, whether from abuse and/or neglect, or the underlying sense of loss from being removed from their birth family, and begin to move forward in his or her life. This can enable them to voice their own view about their lives, and how they would like to be treated and treat others in their future life. Many other themes of emotional significance for children, can therefore be explored through the park environment.

Examples of how the park can be used:

Creative role – play (ideas).	Themes:
Adventure rescues (lifeboat).	Empowerment
Care after sea exposure.	Nurturing.
Being a train driver with Passengers.	Self-expression.
Using Park Apparatus.	Themes (continued).
Using swings, slides, and merry go-rounds.	Releasing Stress and Tensions.
Using climbing apparatus	Building therapeutic Relationship/ self Esteem.
Balancing apparatus	developing focus and Purpose/ handling Pressure.

Using scooters/bikes in skate parks	Releasing anger. Empowerment. Developing peer Confidence after Bullying.
Observing other children (positive play). Engaging with other children.	Restorative sense from past neglect.
Making sand constructions in sand pit or playing with other children.	sharing with others/ Working as a team

Relevant Environments for the Child

Introduction

The third section does not focus on a precise environmental context such as the seashore or the park, but relates to a variety of landscapes determined by a sense of value placed on them by the young person. This can relate to the child's memories of being with his birth family, or with being with his friends, or what he or she may be used to culturally. Alternatively, the child may wish to choose an environment, which is completely different and offers a fresh stimulus for their future life. The therapist or support worker will need to be very sensitive to the choice of the child, which may go in a different direction to a professional sense of acceptability.

This is otherwise known as being 'on the edge of awareness', or just beyond the therapist's comfort zone, or what is consciously expected by them to happen; it is almost like being in the unknown, or unexplored territory, but for the child can fit exactly into their sense of reality and how they can freely both be themselves and move forwards in their lives. This can facilitate the sense of trust between therapist and young person, indicating that he or she really is being 'child centred'. Equally the therapist needs to be completely satisfied that this new environment is both safe, and one in which he/she has some sense of feeling 'ok' in. In this third section, the focus is on a single case study to illustrate this approach.

Val Woskett, in her book 'The Therapeutic Use of Self (Routledge, 1999)', speaks of the value of intuitive and unorthodox work which takes the therapist and client away from the original confines of training or acceptability'. It may be a challenging step to move further into the child's world, which may nevertheless, as Woskett indicates provide an increase in the clients sense of safety and being supported.

CASE STUDY: JACK

INTRODUCTION

This case study is about a young person whom I worked with, called Jack, whose main areas of environmental security, were based on a cemetery, a ten -pin bowling centre, a family pub, and hills and moorland. Although this may seem a very unusual combination of environments for therapeutic engagement, it fitted exactly into what was needed by the young person to feel safe, and through this, express deep and very painful feelings. This allowed him to move forward in his life. Three of the four areas related into his past life, and one, hills and moor land, although linking to his past memories, was a new and exciting departure of experience for him.

I worked with Jack over 4 years, with a first phase of sessions of nearly 2 years, where I built up trust with him, before it emerged, after a short period of time that a further second phase of sessions, would be needed to support him further therapeutically. This proved to be also for nearly 2 years.

This third section relates specifically to the second phase of our sessions, over the two years. It therefore differs from the above two chapters which covered different children and young people, whom I worked with over both short and medium phases of time.

The approach pursued with him, relates to complex trauma models, in which the brain of the young person traumatised, if not able to integrate into his or her past experience, through other approaches, can follow a normalising treatment exposure, in which they are linked to familiar places, and can re-experience the trauma process, but in a safe setting for them, with supportive professionals. This may prove to be a releasing experience, and may be an alternative way of helping young people from more formalised treatment in a hospital or therapy centre. The following section is also a narrative, alongside an applied process of therapy, which links into the issues of self-harm for Jack.

This young person was in foster care, and while our sessions were running, he had been involved in a sudden breakdown of his placement. He was previously happy in his birth family, until his father, whom he was very attached to, suddenly had a stroke, and needed to be cared for by him at home. His mother had just left the home and became involved with another man. After a period of time, his mother came back to the family home, after his father went into nursing care, and her new partner insisted that he was to take charge. Jack was very unhappy about this, and roamed the streets, which led to him being taken into care. His father's parents had passed away, with whom he had been close, and he felt a real sense of responsibility for his family, alongside both sadness and anger with his mother for leaving his father for another man, and not being present at home to care for him.

Jack, as mentioned above, had seen me previously for two years for a first series of sessions, and then was recommended to see me for further sessions, at the time of his foster placement difficulties. Therefore, there may be an initial process of trust needed, lasting quite a long time, before the young person is able to have the confidence to express which type of environment he is comfortable to engage in i.e. in his framework of thinking, could his choice really be accepted, or would it be rejected! This may be very relevant for special needs children too, who have suffered traumatic experiences.

At the outset of our new sessions, Jack mentioned that he felt very angry that he had to clean up his foster family's home while they were away, and felt he was not helped in the home, but given orders instead. This resonated painfully with his past experience (from his perception) of his mother's new partner. There was also a conflict for him, because he partly was getting to the age of independence (he was nearly 18), but also felt attached to his foster carers too. This also linked to his earlier life, in which he had to take responsibility for his father, but at the same time missed being looked after by his parents. A little later he expressed a much deeper sadness saying, 'I wanted my mum to ask me back (while with her new partner) and she didn't, and I felt angry and sad about this'. He seemed happier after being able to express his deeper feelings.

Familiar Landmarks

After seeing his mother for contact, he asked me to take him to where he grew up and said how sad he felt that the shops he remembered as a boy were no longer there, and boarded up, especially the shop where his father worked. He went on to say, that he used to come home from school and help his father, and his mother would help too. Jack had a very positive feeling about his early life, which I said, was a happy aspect to look back on and that perhaps this could be perceived as a jewel or treasure. He reacted well to this, and found it valuable looking around his previous home-town environment. It stimulated both very clear memories and clarity of sentiment, for the following four environments.

The Cemetery (First Phase)

Following this, during the same session, I was due to drop him off to see his father, who was being cared for locally. However, on the way he asked whether we could stop and see his grandmother's grave in a nearby cemetery. He found it very hard to locate the grave, and found it hard to remember her full name, which he had previously, and this precipitated a very deep release of grief, as he felt able to express his pain in tears. This was a moving time, and there were no words spoken, until he felt able to share, that he was not told of his grandmother's passing until after she died, and that he had to be accompanied to the funeral service by Social Services, which he found difficult. He went on to say that all he wanted to do was sit next to his brothers, and that he had not seen his grandmother for a long time while she was alive. There was a deep sense of loss coming through, and helplessness from him.

This was a powerful environmental connection for the young person, which allowed him to share very difficult and painful emotions.

THE TEN-PIN BOWLING CENTRE

In a subsequent session, he asked to visit a ten-pin bowling centre, which he said, was somewhere he felt at ease, and spoke (in the quiet area) about his work in his foster placement not being appreciated, and that no one said, thank you. He felt very angry about this, as he spoke, and I asked him whether this was affecting him in its own right or whether the love and care which he had not been able to receive from his mother and father (more recently), was surfacing up. He nodded emphatically, and was moved, as we both sat in silence.

He went on to say, that he had rung his mother up and spoke of how much his brothers missed her, and wanted to see her, and that it was hard hearing her say that she did not feel that she could see them. Jack spoke of feeling very angry with her, as he wanted to bring his family back together, and that he felt pushed away. He also spoke of his concern for his father, whom he said was quite poorly, and hardly able to recognise him. This was very distressing for him, along with the pressure of feeling responsible for arranging his dad's funeral, as his father had asked him to do this.

There was a harmonious background noise from the bowling alleys, while he was talking, which seemed to facilitate his social confidence, alongside enough space in the coffee area, before it became busy in the later evening, to ensure a sense of privacy and being heard by myself.

He also released presenting tensions, when throwing bowls down the alley, which seemed to build our rapport, before talking.

Jack went on to say how upset he felt that he could not say goodbye to his grandmother, and that there were things he would like to have said to her, and that he wanted to be able to say goodbye to her now. This was a very strong feeling within him, though I also recognised a growing inner strength in him as he was speaking and releasing his pain. There was also very good eye contact.

Jack began to smile a little, and then felt able to say that he had felt it was his entire fault that his family broke up, and even when people said it wasn't he couldn't believe this. He wanted to let me know, that he had been self-harming, showing me red pressure points and that not being able to do anything to change things made him feel it was his fault, but he could at least do something, to himself i.e. self-harm.

He then asked to play pool, and went on to say that playing pool with me helped him somehow, and that a part of him felt it wasn't actually his fault,-what could I have done to stop it, he added,-and a part of him felt it was. I suggested that possibly the part of him, which thinks it is his fault, wants the other part, which doesn't, to take the lead. He reacted well to this and asked to throw a stone on a local beach to symbolise, beginning to let go of his sense of responsibility, and being able to say that it wasn't all, his fault.

In our next session, Jack asked to return to the bowling centre, and was keen to speak about his relationship with his foster carer. He chose a quiet part of the café, and felt at ease with the background noises, and atmosphere. He quickly shared that he had told his foster carer that he had reached his limit with his way of speaking to him, and that his foster carer said that he had reached his limit with him too. He added that he found this honesty really helpful. He was finding it easier to express his real feelings.

After then releasing his sense of anger towards his mother's partner (in our session) he spoke of the importance to him of our visit to the cemetery, and that on our first visit it was hard to say goodbye to his grandmother because there were other people there. The sense of privacy was significant for him during our second visit when he released how he really felt.

He then felt able to express further painful memories, that he was hit by his mother's new partner, and that he could not believe she brought someone into the house straight after his father was taken into hospital, which he found impossible to handle. Jack was then able to express how he felt towards his mother and her partner, which he found empowering.

Following this he seemed a lot less pressurised, and said that what upset him most of all was not saying goodbye to his grandfather and grandmother before they passed away. I asked him, if he was really angry with himself, and he said that he was. This too seemed to release further tensions within him, and he was able to respond to me whilst we were talking in the café area, with a very open question: How can I move on from this guilt and anger I am feeling about myself, concerning my grandma? This showed a lot of self-awareness from Jack, who was quite traumatised by his past life, and who had also suffered panic attacks. This question also showed enormous trust in the person working with him myself which was facilitated by journeying with him in therapeutic spaces which may seem very unorthodox, such as a tenpin bowling centre, but which he felt very secure in.

I suggested to Jack, whether he would like to write a letter to his grandparents expressing his feelings, and what he would like to thank them for. This I added would give him a chance to say 'goodbye to them'. In an instant, he said, I'll get a piece of paper from the bowling people, and walked quickly to a member of staff, who gave him a paper and pen.

There was again a quiet atmosphere, although there may have been a situation where such a special moment may not have been possible, in which case an intervention to a young person to change the venue, or time, may be very appropriate. However, the conditions felt right for him, and I said, that this was a very special time in which we wouldn't talk, and also that he need not show me his letter. Jack, responded very well to this, and silently wrote his deepest conveyance of love for his grandparents. He then asked, if he could burn the letter outside, in a symbolic sense of release, which we did discreetly and carefully. After this he said, that he felt he had made a stepping-stone forwards now, and was happier.

THE FAMILY INN (FIRST PHASE)

When we next met, he asked to go to a local family pub, which he knew of, where he spoke of having to leave his foster family. This session took place, during a morning, when the pub was quiet, and there was minimal noise disruption. Jack was very upset, and spoke of the suddenness of having to leave, being very hard for him, as he liked his new family (in spite of the challenges), and they had been very supportive for a long time. He did not share the reasons for having to go. He went on to say, that leaving their home reminded him of when he was abandoned, by his family, on the streets, and that he felt right back where he started.

This was a similar dynamic to the young person earlier (Philip), inspired by the sea, in which an upheaval in his foster placement, resulting in him having to leave, resonated with the trauma of feeling abandoned by his birth family. Therefore a disruption in foster care can have a double impact on these young people i.e. disruption in care multiplied by disruption with their birth family, and make it much harder for them to function, both in their placements and at school. It may be that this is more significant as an addition relates to an adding on of pain, or 'in proportion' pain, whereas it is possibly more likely that a double quantity of pain (foster care and birth family rejection) opens out an accelerated sense, or 'lots of', released emotions e.g. 5 x 5 rather than 5 add 5.

In the case of these two young people their mother's left the family home. These were probably their main attachment figures. Their father's were left with the main caring role, though this soon stopped, with one father leaving the country, and the young person being brought up initially by his grandparents (Philip), and the other young person's (Jack) father being taken into care himself, for medical reasons. Jack had no living grandparents, and had to run the home himself before living mainly on the streets. This, as mentioned above, resulted in him being taken into care. These reflections are only as I write now, and for both young people led to very powerful and painful emotions emerging.

I responded to Jack,-in the session in the family pub-, that he had come a long way in understanding, and that he was showing a resilience and strength of character in being able to talk about this. He felt it was helpful saying how he really felt, and that he felt comfortable in the pub, and significantly, added that he could be himself.

He was able to recall events leading up to his removal from his care placement (this may have felt completely justified from the viewpoint of his carers, and may have prevented a situation worsening), mentioning that he had been out for the night, and not been able to contact his carers to let them know where he was, and when he returned home the next day he went up to his room, and saw his carer packing his bags. He went on to say, that when he saw this there was nothing he could say, and he ended up in a residential support centre; somehow this young person had the inner strength to speak of feeling positive and nervous about the days ahead. Jack also found it valuable having space to talk about this disruption in his care, and being in an environmental setting, which he was comfortable in e.g. the family pub, facilitated this.

He shared that it was the shock of his carers' reactions which most affected him, and that he had expected to be told off, and no more, and again spoke of the conflict within him that he wanted to move on but also felt very attached to them, and didn't want to move on. This sense of shock was a similar theme to Philip's reactions, which also linked to different expectations from their carers, of the consequences of their behaviour i.e. they felt their behaviour or issues warranted either talking about with them or an appropriate punishment, but did not have on their agenda removal from their placement. They were also unable to fully understand the pressures, which their carers faced in looking after them.

In a subsequent session at the family pub, Jack spoke of self-harming himself through pinching, both at night and during the day, and that he wanted staff at the centre to know about this, as he was feeling bad about himself that he had not seen his father for 3 months. The self-harming for him was a signal of communication to others, as to how he was feeling, when his self-esteem was very low. He had promised his father, he added, that he would see him every week; his father was in a residential care setting after, as mentioned above, having suffered a stroke.

Intervening therapeutically can also be very helpful, for young people, and I spoke of him being a good and caring son for his father and that there were bound to be times when he had his own pressures, and would not be able to see him. He listened carefully, and said 'lets have a game of pool'!

In the following session, he asked to return to the same family pub, and said that he was feeling very wound up, and wanted to ask his mother why she abandoned him. This had been, he went on to say, burning up inside of him like a volcano, and that people in the centre were asking why he was self-harming, and were very concerned for him. At the same time he chose some music to listen to, in the Inn, while we sat in silence. The lyrics of the music were very important to him.

After a while I asked him, if he was self-harming because he was angry more with his mother than himself now, and wanted her to appreciate and suffer his pain too. He replied that this was so, and asked me whether he should show her what he had done to himself. There was a sense, that he wanted his mother to know what was happening to him, and perhaps to take responsibility for what she had done. I re-enforced to him that he was special in his own way, and challenged him that he should not have to suffer for how he was treated, and hurt himself, to express this, and that he could express his pain by sharing how he felt to me (I had known him for over a year at this point), instead of hurting himself.

Following this Jack stared straight at me with direct eye contact, for a few minutes, without talking, and then seemed much less tense, and asked to listen to more music. He went up to choose his favourite music, which we listened to (again in silence), which spoke of carrying pain. There was no dialogue at this time, after which he suddenly said that I, and some of his friends had prevented him taking his own life.

This was a longer therapeutic session, than planned, and it may sometimes occur that the therapist in these situations will need flexibility to accommodate the explosion of powerful feelings at the moment, which feels right to a young person. Jack seemed much more relaxed after this, speaking of a friend at the centre who he liked and could have a laugh with, along with listening to the music of Pink Floyd, in which, he added, he related the lyrics of their songs very closely to his feelings about his family. This also seemed a key ingredient for him at the Inn, where he could reflect quietly in a much deeper way about his family, as he listened to his choice of music. This was a very safe mechanism for self-reflection, and processing traumatic events.

THE CYCLE TRAIL (FIRST PHASE)

We were due to see his mother for contact, on Saturday (Jack saw her alone for one hour), and he asked if he could go for a cycle ride on a cycle trail, for the first time afterwards, to cope with things. This was because he was worried, he said, if he really shared how he felt that she would be angry and not wish to see him again. The pain of further rejection was very acute for him, as we made gentle steps to begin to restore their relationship, which was his desire.

His situation was further stimulated by the return of his belongings in the week from his former foster placement, which may also have stirred, his sense of abandonment, and rejection. I suggested that he may wish to think carefully about the right moment to share this with his mother, and that if this wasn't right on this occasion he could continue to share his feelings with me.

Jack found it wasn't appropriate to talk with his mother about this, and was very keen to experience cycling on the trail afterwards. This was a refreshing experience for him, in strong winds, and near an estuary, and allowed him to release the intensity of his time at contact. He spoke for the first time of wanting to achieve cycling along the trails whole length, and we agreed to build up the distance, on separate sessions, to achieve this. I felt it was encouraging that for the first time he focused on something, which he could achieve, beyond the traumatic events of his past. This was facilitated by his sense of identification with this trail, from his past family cycle outings, as 'a happy place'.

This was another significant time where a link with a familiar environment, prompted a past happy experience, after being able to release more traumatic events from his past, in previous sessions. There was perhaps the beginning of an 'integration' for him with his past, encompassing the traumatic phases.

THE FAMILY INN (SECOND PHASE)

In a following session, meeting at the family Inn, during a morning where there were few customers, and in the pool room, where Jack felt most able to share traumatic events (no one else was present, but background music was heard), he spoke of a remarkable change in his family situation, having seen his mother in mid week. He was able to express to her that being in foster care was not what he wanted, and this allowed her to say, he added, that she never wanted this to happen and that he was a special son to her. This clearly meant so much to him. He was also seeking to build a positive relationship with her new partner, who was interested in his family pictures. He went on to show me too, his family pictures on his mobile, and said that he had stopped self-harming since seeing his mother, and felt a happier person.

This seemed to allow him to process further traumatic events from his past, and during a subsequent session, at the same venue, he spoke of having a flashback in his current placement triggered by a play fight, with a friend, who he allowed to hit him, until it triggered a past event of someone hitting him, and that he really hit out at his friend who was shocked. However, they made up very quickly, he added.

Jack said how disturbed he felt by the flash back. I asked him, 'what was said', and 'how it began', and he felt able to recall that he was downstairs with his mother's partner, and his brothers were upstairs and heard raised voices, and that he was upset that his mother was not paying him any attention, as she always used to, and didn't speak. He felt this was due to her partner, and after explaining this to him, Jack asked him to leave. Following this, he was (he added), beaten up by her partner.

This connected for Jack with what happened with his friend, and through this understanding, he became more relaxed. He went on to express his anger with his mother's partner, and that he felt completely helpless that he could not help his mother, from her partner's control.

I asked him, if he was angry with himself, and he said that he was, showing me a graze where he had hit a wall the previous night, because of his anger.

There were no distractions as he spoke and there were the two cues nearby resting on the pool table, ready to be used if he wished. I affirmed that he was a young person then who could not be expected to have changed his family situation, and was brave to have spoken out. At this point, his body language seemed to change, and he smiled saying that he was "feeling stronger, like a coil being unwrapped".

Although there was a subsequent phase of time where Jack returned to self-harming when his mother didn't respond to his calls, through talking he was able to process that this could be linked to issues affecting her rather than about him, including not having credit on her phone to respond. He also began to reflect more, about how his mother could be feeling, rather than act on impulse, and decided to write her a letter, to give a voice to his pain and what he described as torment. This moved away from the immediacy of pressure of the phone. He also felt able to speak about seeing his father too, and reading him a story, and then speaking to him about their early family memories. This meant a lot to Jack, who shared how his father didn't seem to remember-he had suffered a serious stroke -, but that with prompts from him, he remembered. He was very encouraged and felt much more empowered now.

I asked him to voice what he would like to say to her, and he said that he wanted to say how much her lack of contact was affecting him, and that he appreciated they had 16 good years together. Subsequently he met his mother, and this was a positive experience, in which he felt able to ask her why she couldn't return his calls.

THE CEMETERY (SECOND PHASE)

He then asked to visit the cemetery again, in our session, where he released his sadness for not being there when his paternal grandparents passed away, and with support, his appreciation for all they had done for him, a moving thank you, leading him to say 'goodbye'. This brought a special closure to him, and an opportunity to move forwards in his life. We had also visited where they used to live, and the happy memories, which this brought him, including where his grandfather kept his hats. This brought a further integration of his past life, and the key attachment figures that impacted him. I felt this also gave him a strong sense of identity with his father's side of the family, through powerful environmental life connections.

This was a real step forward for him, and led to the next phase of expression at the family pub, of feeling very worried for his mother and her welfare, and that he should be caring for her. He was now able to understand his behaviour much quicker, explaining that he self harmed again because he was not happy with himself. I encouraged him to give consideration to his mother being an adult, even though it was very natural to be concerned, and she could seek help from other people if she needed to. He was very relieved after hearing this.

The Family Inn (Third Phase)

In a further session, he spoke of the environment of sitting down in the inn, next to the pool table, being where he felt most relaxed, breaking from his game, half way through. This led to him sharing a further traumatic time, when his father had a stroke and how this affected him, when coping with it alone in his house, and the deep feelings of loneliness and pain, which he felt at the time. He also, in further sessions released situations of aggression and violence, which were very traumatic for him, and which he could now talk about, releasing his anger, without hurting himself.

Listening to Music

Since then, a closer relationship grew between Jack and his mother, confirmed by a call from her to him, and in a further session, at the inn, he chose to play a song, from the juke box, which his grandfather always listened to, when they stayed with him. Listening to music was a very important way for Jack to release his grief, and get in touch with himself, and his feelings and memories of his grandfather in a deeper way, which also felt very safe for him. After listening to the song, he spoke to me of, his father quickly waking him to say that his grandfather was going to pass away, and that he missed saying goodbye to him. After a period of silence, he shared that his grandfather previously placed on his hand a special ring, which he said, was to remember him by, and which he would like him to keep. The young person spoke of finding it difficult to take the ring initially, as it had such special significance to his grandfather.

Following this he looked directly at me, and asked me to place my hand palm upwards, in front of me, and he placed this ring on the palm of my hand, and said, my grandfather gave it to me like this. There was a sense, of Jack wanting me to understand how significant this was for him, though also that he wanted me to enter in a deeper way of empathy, and be there with him, in the depth of feeling he had at that time, and now. There was an implicit sense that he was expressing that this was his special time with him. I also encouraged him to re-think what happened too, and to consider that he had been able to say goodbye to his grandfather in this special way. He responded with a quiet smile, with no further discussion.

Symbolically, these therapeutic sessions were like a journey on a boat together, where there were many rapids and turbulence, along with periods of calm, before Jack finally reached towards the wide calm estuary.

THE CYCLE TRAIL (SECOND PHASE): CHANGE OF FOCUS

During the latter phase of our sessions, he asked to cycle again along the cycle trail, after seeing his mother, and shared that this helped him to clear his head, and that he needed to do this. He spoke of a happy family experience along it, with his mother and her partner, and his brothers, in which a family member took a photograph, just as he fell over his bike! He was smiling as he spoke, and spoke of them all laughing together when they looked at the photograph. To be able to share this meant a lot to him. We also engaged in further cycling trips where the main focus, for him, became not the traumatic events of his past life, but being able to achieve set targets of distance, which would give him a sense of achievement. Although physical tiredness was a challenging battle, he achieved progressively further distances in each session, until reaching his end destination. This he expressed made him feel proud of himself, and what he could now do in his life.

Shortly after this Jack moved into a family foster care situation, where he felt happy and settled. Although the love and care which he received, touched into the sense of absence, of what he wished for from his own family and there were painful phases, he persevered, with the strong support of his foster family, and made a lot of progress. He was also able to release this painful conflict within our sessions, and go beyond it in a mountain and moor environment.

SEEING HIS FATHER

He had mentioned to me, during the early phase of his placement that he had self-harmed again, on his arm, which he said was under his control, to take the pain away of missing his family. I introduced that being in a caring foster family again, would touch into the sense of family, which he used to have, and that the loss of that family would be a grief for him. Therefore in beginning to understand his feelings, he could be equipped more to make meaningful choices i.e. to choose not to self-harm. He related well to this, and I added, that what was affecting him was a hard but good way through, with his pain being touched in a positive family environment. I encouraged him to allow himself to hear this, and avoid the choice of self-harming. He reflected quietly on this, and indicated he was thinking about this already, asking suddenly if he could climb a mountain and become fitter, and achieve something in his life.

On the day of our session, when he was due to climb his first moorland peak with me, he was very distressed because he had not had an opportunity to visit his father for two months, and had been self-harming again. Jack spoke again of the pain of not being able to do anything about his father's situation or help him, which was causing him to cut himself to take the pain away. He had also not received any texts back from his mother, though also, even in his very painful situation, he added that his mother was there sometimes for him like his foster carers were for him now. There seemed even in tough moments, an underlying strength emerging.

Jack asked me, if he could see his father-which we followed through-, instead of climbing a peak. I was aware how important it was for him, and took him to see his father, and waited outside, as he always saw him alone. Although anxious beforehand, he came out with a huge sense of relief, and was much happier.

In the following session, Jack was very keen to climb the same peak, and having fulfilled seeing his father was emotionally able to move forward with his goals.

Therefore, where a presenting pressure connects to past trauma, unless this is resolved (as much as possible), it can block the underlying desires of the young person, and his own self-development.

Moorland Peak

As we were walking up to his first introductory peak, he was struck by the peace and quietness of the moors, and noticed a foal with his mother, which prompted him to say that he was hurting because he couldn't see the rest of his family (i.e. nephew and nieces), and precisely explaining his frustration: I text my brothers and they just don't reply, so I cut myself. The visual image of the foal with its mother impacted him at a deeper level, and he related it quickly into his own sense of loss. Although, as we were reaching the top, Jack spoke of wanting to text a message to his brothers to tell them he was hurting, he also said that somehow now he didn't need to hurt himself with his mother and father any more, saying "that's gone now".

I also introduced, while at the summit (385 metres) that he can release pain in situations like this i.e. through talking, which he was doing, rather than on himself. He listened carefully, whilst observing the views for miles around. He also smiled and said 'I have achieved my goal, and have lost weight, and can now think of myself as someone who is doing something in my life. He asked me if he could climb another hill, another time.

In the following session, Jack shared that he had now applied for an access course at a local college, and was nervous and excited, and that he was getting on well with his foster dad. I also encouraged him to consider beginning to let go slightly of those members of his family, who were not responding to him, as he had played his part in seeing them, and focusing more on his own life. I also challenged him to help his foster mum, with a more positive attitude, which he listened to.

ACHIEVING HIS GOAL

After this, in our next session, he asked to return to the cycle trail, where he succeeded in achieving his goal of completing the ride from beginning to end, overcoming tiredness, and presenting concerns. A key aspect was that he had previously completed two thirds of it, and he knew he was in a position to win his battle, before starting. He reacted well to encouragement, along with breaks to build up energy again. Jack also looked back on the trip, and reflected in past tense, that he had been able to grieve for his grandparents while we spoke and cycled the trail. He had the opportunity to talk about them, during the challenge, and express his love from them, and how he just wanted them back. This seemed releasing for him.

When we next met Jack spoke to me, of the sad death of his father whom he was devoted to, and how in the sadness at the hospital, he was able to speak to him, and share that his family were at last all together again. He knew his father was listening even though he couldn't answer back. This meant a lot to him, as he supported his wider family, and expressed his relief, in our session, that there was no more suffering for his father.

He also said that he was accepted by a local college for an access course, although a little anxious. There was a reference to possible self-harming, linked to the uncertainty of whether his mother would come to the funeral service, and wanting her to see the pain he had felt for his father, though he was also encouraged in their relationship now.

Jack through understanding loss much more now, and how this affected him, and also being able to process his past traumas, through environmental therapy, developed the inner strength and resources to cope with the loss of his father, and beyond that support his brothers. He was growing through it into a place of emerging strength emotionally, though still in need of caring support.

As he was soon to reach the age of 18, the authorities asked me to begin a smooth transition to adult services for him, very gently suggesting our sessions would need in the next few months to come to a close. At the same time, I was able to attend a transition meeting with him, with the adult psychology service, to provide continuity. I was also asked to share key aspects of my work during another meeting, to help further continuity with adult psychology. This only happened with Jack's agreement. He previously refused to see anyone professional in a formal context. This transition soon led to him attending monthly meetings without me, while I began to bring our sessions to a sensitive close. The settled foster placement, which he had, was also a very key ingredient to facilitate this, where Jack felt happy and secure. He also asked me if I would attend his father's funeral, which I did.

Following this, in our next session, Jack asked to walk the same cycle trail, where he spoke of his mother and himself coming closer together now through his dad's death. He was also keen to share with me, that he was with his father throughout a previous day in hospital, just before he died, and what meant most to him, was that when he was most distressed and upset, a lady came and hugged him. Her husband was passing away, and he added, that she said to him, I know what you are going through. He spoke of how much this helped him.

Placing very challenging events in Perspective

In our penultimate session, Jack asked to climb another summit in the same moorland area. There was a quiet and soothing remoteness to this environment, in which he spoke of his sadness of the passing of his father and that he wished he could come back. I listened and spoke of a special word during the funeral service, by the vicar, of his father being generous to help anyone, which he identified with and smiled. He went on to speak, while at the summit (390 metres), of being able to see his nephew, and being asked by him where his grandfather was, and being able to say, he's gone to a better place. There was a depth to Jack, as he was speaking, where he seemed to really enjoy being at the top of the hill, and sharing he felt 'above his world and its problems', and that being here "helped him to clear his head". His body language was of a person much more settled and confident in himself. On the descent, he was much more at ease with the different animals on the moor, and was touched by a young foal with its father, walking very closely alongside each other, and saying "that his father would be very proud to see him do this", which was a special way of almost finishing our time together.

There was a real depth to his observations of the animals of this environment, which helped this young person to reach a deeper resonance with the loss in his own life, and through this positively release his deeper feelings with a supportive person alongside.

This approach could be used as a medium of expression, with some young people, related to trauma exposure treatment. This young person did not speak of any self-harming during the last three months, which may link with a greater sense of empowerment in his life, through talking and practical solutions e.g. achieving goals.

He returned to presenting concerns, speaking of looking forward to his college course, and being supportive to his foster mother, and how he appreciated the love and care of both his foster carers, and asking if we could both visit the grave of his father now, as a final goodbye to him. This was very moving, and seemed to help in a profound way, as he brought a sense of closure to his father's passing. In our last session, Jack asked to meet with his friends in a local church social setting, in which he asked me to join him, which was a very appropriate time to finish our therapeutic engagement. I see him occasionally at his foster carers for a short time, though not for therapeutic engagement, and he has presented as well and happy, though without full engagement with his family, which he has come to accept.

Conclusion

In terms of analysis, although this has a narrative aspect, it allows the reader to understand the depth of pain which the young person went through, and how using different safe environments was a way he could both, safely engage in his past trauma, and feel secure enough to, process its implications and affects emotionally on him as a person. This gave him both the emotional strength and stability to express himself, and understand why he was reacting and behaving as he was; it also allowed him to begin to identify a sense of his own life having enough significance to achieve personal goals and achievements, though initially this needed to be in a familiar environment. This led him to begin to develop his own sense of identity, and look forwards in his life to new environmental horizons, such as a new college course, which he was looking forward to. Throughout this process a stable and caring foster placement was a vital ingredient for him.

Outdoor Development

Introduction

This fourth section focuses on the role of the outdoor environment to enhance the self-confidence of the child or young person, in terms of therapeutic change. This was brought out in the above section, through the young person, identifying environments that were special to him. However, the difference, in focusing on outdoor development, is that it can also be identified or suggested by the therapist, as an initiative, which may not have occurred to the child or young person. In the case of my own background, I have been trained and qualified as a Mountaineering Party Leader (MLA), and as a Canoe England Coach (K2), and therefore to give an opportunity for traumatised young people to express themselves both in skill development, and experientially, in the above outdoor arenas, seemed worth pursuing.

Therapists with other outdoor skills can equally be used, or consideration given by them to train and qualify in different outdoor disciplines, which could add a completely new dimension to their therapeutic contribution. It could also allow them to be seen by a young person, as a role model, which may provide a sense of direction for them which they have been seeking all their lives. In other words being led by the child, may not work for all young people, and offering purposeful direction, can allow more of their potential to be released.

Alternatively, some therapists could work alongside an outdoor instructor, with the young person, experiencing what they go through, without needing to have a background in an outdoor discipline. This perhaps has an advantage that both the young person and the therapist are going through outdoor experiences together, experientially at the same level, which could facilitate a positive therapeutic bond between them; in other words, they are facing the outdoor world and its challenges together, and this process could allow a young person to feel a reality with his therapist. This may then help him to talk about painful areas of his life.

Also, there can be many opportunities to engage in outdoor activities, which do not require specialist qualifications, and therefore a therapist and the young person could go cycling or walking for example, having a shared experience, which could be very valuable in developing trust and rapport between them. This could also provide a sense of normality, for the young person, which could then allow him to have a positive context, within which to explore traumatic areas or phases of his life.

Three examples of using specialist skills from canoeing, are shown below. This is also written for those in the outdoor industry to consider the therapeutic benefits of the outdoor environment, as well as encouraging professionals involved in therapy, to apply any outdoor skills. I also applied skills as a Mountaineering Leader with the young person in the above section of this book, relating to planning and navigation, in a mountain and moorland context.

Three Case Studies

Case Study One: Loss

I took one young person, called Roger whom I had been working with for over one year, for one star kayaking sessions, in a very calm inlet of an estuary. Roger had responded well to this opportunity, and enjoyed water sports generally. He was aged 14, and had witnessed violence between his mother and father, alongside feeling a real sense of loss since his father and mother separated, and his father went to live abroad. This resulted in him seeing his father very rarely. He also felt a sense of responsibility for his mother, whom he felt was suffering as a single parent.

This young person, as we travelled to the kayaking location, spoke of seeing his father last week, and that he really enjoyed his time with him, though he also felt a sadness that he had to go back, and that it would be a long time before he saw him again. He identified, that this was probably why he was feeling low, though added that he was looking forward to taking his mother to see a comedy film tonight. I had been focusing in the last year, on ways in which the young person could express more of how he felt about his family life, and also how he and his mother could relax more, with a sense of fun, to build their relationship, rather than just having tensions linked to the realities of economic survival.

In our canoeing session, Roger responded well to a more directive approach of being taught how to forward paddle and turn the kayak, and observed carefully these canoe demonstrations, before applying them him self. He seemed very relaxed, and shared that 'the texture of the water was very calming'. He was also fascinated by the serenity and closeness of a group of swans, and their togetherness seemed to impact him. He paddled close to them. The peacefulness of the swan's family life, was a valuable insight for him, when there had often been considerable tensions in his own family life. He also completed a figure of eight course to apply the above skills, and was pleased with what he had achieved. On the way home, he mentioned that he felt peaceful, like when he went surfing,

In a subsequent session, Roger asked if we could go canoeing again, and spoke on the way, of the pressure of school life, and the lessons being boring, and home life being difficult as he felt his mother was 'going on at him'. I felt there was an underlying dissatisfaction within Roger, and asked him, whether he was really missing his father. He reacted very quickly indeed with anger, responding that his father had chosen to go and live with a foreign lady (instead of being with himself), and that he could get affected by all the smoking he did. This young person was suffering from strong rejection, along with a sense of responsibility for his family. I was aware he had visited his father and his new partner abroad, and asked if she was supportive when he travelled to see his father. He said, that he never had time alone with his father when he was there, and there were always others around. I affirmed how well he had done to express deeper and more painful feelings, and that as he learnt to understand how his anger and sadness were related to missing his father, this could help him to let go of the 'low feelings', and begin to move forwards in his life.

This seemed to make sense to him, and he suddenly said in a lighter tone, that it would be good to go canoeing and he would like both instruction, and a sense of fun, from this activity. This perhaps mirrored or reflected what he most desired in his own life, from his father, which was achieved only when his father came to see him. He wished deeply that he could have this sort of relationship with his father throughout his adolescent years, rather than for very limited periods of time.

I taught him further forward paddling skills in this canoe session, and then asked him to paddle in a circle in a controlled manner. Following this he suddenly, lay flat, at an angle, in his kayak, and looked up at the sky. As this was a therapeutic experience too, it was very appropriate to run with this, as he focused on the clouds in silence. It seemed as if he was able to let go of all the presenting pressures of his life at this time, possibly along with a restorative dimension to his deeper sadness. There were no human sounds, or distractions. Roger then noticed a plane going across the sky and was struck by its speed. He was very aware of distance and air travel through visiting his father abroad. I felt he had an engagement with the water, which was very calming and supportive, as he was able to float in his kayak, with little wind. He also found it valuable to touch the water with his hands, and engage with it through the movement of his fingers. I reflected whether this symbolised the need, in a sensory way, for a close relationship with his father.

The challenge for me was to balance this vital aspect with a focus orientation on the skills, which he wished to gain. However, after touching the water in silence with his whole self involved, he suddenly said, 'how much more do I need to learn to get the one star award?' I felt the sense of choice he was having, even within focused therapeutic work was very important still. It allowed him to reach the deeper sense of restoration, which he needed, through looking up at the clouds and touching the water. There followed a complete transformation in his motivational outlook to achieve his goal. In other words because he was able to make his own choice to look at the clouds, this empowered him, with the energy, to reach goals for his own life. This was the opposite of his family situation, in which he felt helpless to restore the breakdown of his family life, and to see his father more.

I then asked him to practice a sculling draw stroke (sideways movement stroke), and after I demonstrated it, he worked very hard to apply this stroke. This was by placing the paddle blade in the water, and pulling it towards his boat, before turning it 90 degrees to the kayak. He then had to move it outwards again, before repeating the stroke. He realised that he was moving sideways in his kayak, and succeeding, and was fulfilling one of the strokes, which he had to fulfil 'the early beginnings of', as it was a two star award stroke. He was very keen to share, that he felt ok with this stroke, and the other strokes, which he had practiced too, asking when could he gain his one star.

This was quite an insight into his underlying desire to achieve in his life. He also carefully observed me demonstrating the stern rudder stroke (a steering stroke), and then even before I had finished, he placed his paddle in a similar position behind the stern, and parallel to his boat, before sweeping the blade in small movements to the right and left, to apply his stroke correctly. I applied this at speed, and he observed and correctly demonstrated his stroke too. His confidence was growing.

Roger then, through his own initiative, edged his kayak with his hips, in a controlled way from one side to the other, without his paddle. This movement fascinated him. It is a confidence boosting technique taught by instructors, and is also applied at 3 star levels. The key aspect was that he could tip the kayak towards the water, as a balance technique, before just pulling back at the right moment of time, or else you fall in! He really enjoyed this balancing experience.

This was a therapeutic link with boundaries, too, in which the young person was testing himself, as far as he felt was right, to edge the canoe towards the water, before pulling back with his hips, and being aware in one sense of staying safe from falling in the water. However, getting wet is also a valuable experience for confidence too! Roger could possibly therefore, begin to appreciate through his own self -created boundaries, with these edging movements, that there is a wider reason for boundaries-to keep us safe and that this is applied in family and school life too, for our benefit. Following this, although there were highs and lows in his family life, he spoke, of things being better at home. This may be an indicator of him making sense of these connections.

I developed this edging initiative, and showed him the low brace support stroke, which has a 'gorilla stance', with the lower arms facing downwards, like a gorilla, to hold the paddle, with the blade placed flat against the water. This is to gain support from the paddle blade when the kayak is edged to the side, as Roger was previously doing without paddle support. He then applied this stroke effectively using the paddle, along with accompanying gorilla sounds and a lot of laughter! It was important too for him to have a strong sense of fun, as he had often taken on parental responsibilities of concern for both his mother and father. He was very worried his father could die from smoking heavily, and wanted to help him to stop, and was concerned that his mother, as the sole parent carer, was shouting too much, and never had any fun in her life. Alongside this he had the pressures of his own life, and concerns for his relationship with his younger brother.

Roger went on to apply this support stroke correctly, on both sides of the kayak, and when I asked him what difference placing the back of the paddle, on the water made, his response was 'more support', which was correct. This young person was making very good progress towards his one star, and was able to apply sweep strokes (turning strokes) on both sides of his kayak correctly, with confidence. He was also able to ask me what a reverse sweep stroke meant, to clarify his own understanding.

At the end of the session, I asked him, his view of the session, and what was most helpful. He shared that it was annoying when I said, 'you're there', (which related to kayak strokes which he had achieved), and then 'you asked me to do the paddle strokes again.' I recognised that there was a positive tone as he spoke! I then asked him, why he thought I asked him to do the stroke again, and he said, "to re-fine it", which I affirmed. Therefore a directive dimension if balanced appropriately, can also be therapeutically valuable for a young person affected by traumatic and distressing events in their life.

He also went on to say that he enjoyed the session, and really liked going around with the sweep strokes, and practicing backwards paddling, which he had learnt in a previous session. I developed this and encouraged him to turn his head as he paddled backwards to develop body rotation, which he responded well to. I was very encouraged in this session, for Roger and its potential affects on his wider life.

Subsequently, he felt things were improving slowly in his life, with regular contact with his father by phone, and his father coming to see him for Christmas. He also successfully passed, in a further session, his one star canoe assessment. He was very happy about this, feeling he had achieved something now in his life. I encouraged him that he was also able to understand himself more now, and recognise his deeper feelings and what causes them i.e. the absence of his father.

Overall, I felt an outdoor approach had a positive therapeutic affect on Roger giving him much more self-belief and purpose in his life.

CASE STUDY TWO: FOCUS

This directional approach also helped another young person, called Elaine who had suffered sexual abuse, and was having to go through a court process. It was felt she could benefit therapeutically from experiencing an activity, such as canoeing, which could release her tensions and anxieties at this time, rather than sessions, which linked into her situation. She was very keen to learn how to paddle, (her female worker also was supporting our sessions, and observing her), and after I explained and demonstrated how to paddle on the shoreline, she found that she could paddle forwards in an ocean kayak. This strengthened her own sense of what she could achieve, and in the following summer she was keen to continue to canoe, and develop her skills. Her court process was still ongoing, and she was aware that she would be involved with cross -examination by barristers.

In the initial session it was very important for Elaine to feel supported, and holding the back or front of her canoe, allowed her to paddle 5 metres forwards and then after explaining how to backwards paddle, by holding onto the paddle blade with her, she was able to paddle backwards independently. This gave her the confidence to progress to learning how to turn the kayak, through sweep strokes, which I demonstrated, and it was very interesting to observe, her facial composure change positively, mid way through the session. When suffering from her abuse, it is very likely she would have felt out of control of her situation, with no one available to support her, and allow her to regain control. Therefore the process of learning how to canoe, alongside two supportive adults, had the very opposite ingredients to facilitate this change. Elaine presented as being very happy, and then felt able to trust myself as her instructor to hold the front of her canoe and gently tip it from side to side, which were the early beginnings of the low brace support stroke. Another key benefit of this approach was building up trust for her in other adults.

The following year she made the decision, to continue canoeing, and after re-enforcing the above strokes, she made the next step to independent canoeing, without the instructor (myself) holding the boat. This was in a small rectangular area within a very sheltered inlet of an estuary. Her female worker, watching from the shoreline, was very positive about this approach, and was able to observe her. Elaine was also able to observe me demonstrating the sweep stroke, as I was standing in the water and sweeping the paddle, with the focus on the blade being immersed in the water for power. This was applied in slow motion. She then applied the sweep strokes independently, and correctly, and made a wide arc movement with her paddle, to give power to the stroke.

For the first time she made an independent observation, saying that a left sweep stroke, or turning stroke, following a right sweep stroke would correct the direction of the boat, from her own experience of paddling. It was encouraging that she could voice what she knew to be right, which she would later have to do in a courtroom. This was empowering for her.

This session, I introduced a variety of boats for her to experience paddling in, and from which she could make an informed choice, concerning the boat or boats, which she most preferred. This included an open canoe, in which the young person paddled in the front, and I steered in the back. Before embarking, I explained to her how to forward paddle. We completed four short circular movements in this inlet, before I went on to explain how to backwards paddle, which she applied correctly. Therefore working as a team, to achieve an objective co-operatively, was an important therapeutic ingredient for her. She spoke of enjoying a variety of paddling experience in different boats.

Elaine continued for a further 4 sessions, regularly spaced out throughout the summer. After each session, the three of us reviewed the session, and what she had achieved, in a positive way. I also felt a positive 'framework' to achieve, could be helpful to her, and therefore introduced the Canoe England Paddle Power scheme (for young people aged under 16). This involves the candidate having set skills which he or she learns, and then when achieved, is recorded, on a special record card, by the instructor. It allows progression over 4 levels, after which the young person achieves a national award equivalent to one star.

Elaine reacted very well to this approach, and was delighted to see herself progress from level 2 to level 4, which allowed her to process that positive change and development was happening in her life, and that she was applying this herself.

It was also important to involve her co-worker, and we next developed precise focusing skills, in forwards and backwards paddling from myself in the water to her co-worker on the bank or shoreline. This developed her accuracy, and also allowed the co-worker some interaction with the young person, as she achieved this objective.

Another part of the award scheme, linked to progression, was for the young person to paddle independently for 200 metres (level 2). Elaine was able to apply this as she paddled close to the shoreline with myself walking alongside her on the bank. This was a breakthrough point, in which she moved out of the smaller rectangular area, and felt delighted to push her own boundaries, to a wider area. This principle would be applicable when going to court and being cross-examined. There was a visible change in her confidence, and on the return leg, she decided to increase speed, and was pleased with the impact this had on her journey. This led Elaine to take a further initiative, in which she said to me, 'you get the open canoe', and we repeated the journey in separate boats. This reflected a more dramatic boost in her confidence level, in which she also applied two sweep strokes to turn her boat, near the harbour wall. She was making a faster rate of progress now. There was also a clear sense of movement in her self belief, and what she could achieve, and I was later informed of the confidence she spoke in the court room to the barrister who cross examined her.

In her last three sessions, I refined her paddle stroke skills, and also introduced capsizing from her boat. This was approached gradually, in which she initially adjusted to floating in the water with her buoyancy aid on, close to shore, leading to jumping from an open ocean kayak, close to shore, and pulling in her boat whilst holding the paddle. She gained an exhilarated sense of achievement from this. Elaine also achieved level 3 of her award, which included a 500 metre journey, and key parts of level 4 in her final session, including more dramatic edging strokes, involving balancing skills, and the beginnings of sculling support in her ocean kayak.

There was an emerging picture of a much more independent person and canoeist, which I felt could have a very positive impact on her life, and the challenges which she had to go through. In the following year, she spoke to her co-worker of the positive impact which canoeing had on her, and how she stood up strongly to cross-examination, leading to the imprisonment of those who abused her.

CASE STUDY THREE: SELF IMAGE

A further example of the impact of outdoor development, therapeutically, through canoeing was on one young person, called Ned who could not adjust to secondary school, and the academic and emotional requirements. He had suffered from severe neglect and was taken into care, and needed to catch up in his life, both on academic levels, and social interaction. He was presenting to his peers, as a much younger person below his chronological age, resulting in him being isolated.

However, he was interested in water sports, and through learning to swim (he went to a swimming instructor with his foster carer) and canoe (with myself) -in which he gained his one star award-, his self confidence in what he could now achieve, changed his view of himself, and he began to believe in himself. This led to him reacting more co-operatively at school, and with strong support from his foster carers, and social care, alongside his school, he developed less need to challenge, and avoid reality, and felt able to reveal more of his real self, and a desire to bring out many strengths that were in his life.

I was able to instruct him for his one star award over 5 sessions, and finding that something was not easy, and needed to be worked at, with commitment, and yet could be achieved, led to him sharing over one year later how much the canoeing meant to him. Ned spoke of how surprised he was when he capsized without this being planned, and was pleased with himself that he reacted calmly and swam with his paddle and canoe, held in one hand, whilst swimming with his legs and other arm band to shore (with myself alongside him). He also spoke of finding it very encouraging that he could paddle in a straight line in his canoe, as part of his one-star training, both forwards and backwards, expressing that this was good i.e. giving him a sense of order and focus. Ned also enjoyed a short canoe journey along the coast with us paddling alongside each other, which allowed him to view different bird life from a new perspective. There was a widening of horizons, for him, which led on to success at school in drama, and a more positive self-image.

Conclusion

Therefore the impact of any work in outdoor development, whichever sport or activity is involved, can lead to many long-term benefits for the young person. The focus in this section has been on canoeing, which is only one of many exciting and beneficial activities e.g. climbing or sailing, which can be introduced.

USING ANIMALS IN THE ENVIRONMENT:

INTRODUCTION

The last section relates to using animals in the environment to benefit young people therapeutically. This emerged for me, when I was simply finding that I could only go so far in verbal dialogue, with those children and young people who were so traumatised by their experiences of abuse and neglect, that it was too painful for them to even think about. It was therefore safer to repress or push down their experiences emotionally, rather than talk. I reflected on other more creative ways of engaging with these young people. This was also because they were finding that even gently put and infrequent questions about what happened to them or how they felt, rather than bring out their trauma and allow them to process it, was causing them irritation or mild anger; it was leading to avoidance or changing the subject very suddenly.

This led to me considering whether using animals could be a vehicle of communication for the child, which felt safe for them to express how they felt without needing to talk, unless they wanted to, and created a sense of an accepting silence. It was like an atmosphere of unconditional understanding or love which did not require a response, but could reach their deepest areas of pain and release their feelings without anxiety that they could be judged, or even that they could be prompted to have to face their own guilt or self-judgment.

I also noted research information about using dogs, discovering that they had a strong sensory dimension, with eyes like a blue bottle fly which can process what they see much quicker than humans e.g.

danger coming, suffering, catching a ball, hearing which allows them to hear sounds more than 4 times further away than humans, with twice as high a pitch, and includes lights humming, and smell which has many more receptors than human beings. One remarkable example of the depth of a dogs smell was a dog who smelt the tumour of his owner, and whose mood suddenly became very low and withdrawn from her. As this continued, his owner became concerned whether this related to herself, and she had a medical screening. Amazingly a cancerous tumour was detected, and then removed from her. She acknowledged afterwards that her life had been saved by her dog's reactions.

Their sense of smell also relates to the distant past, and smells which provoke both positive and negative memories. A simple example is the caution of my own dog Lionel, who looks forward to entering the vet's premises until he picks up the smell of the anaesthetics! Another example was a dog that went into a café and recalled from the smell of the café, a past violent incident, and had an alarmed response. Our own dog, Lionel also came up to my front door when welcoming my niece when visiting with her boyfriend, but hadn't seen them for at least a year. He began to lift his nose and smell them, before wagging his tail in a friendly manner! Their smell therefore relates to their understanding that 'these people are ok'.

There is therefore a profound sensitivity coming from dogs, which allows them to pick up how we may be feeling. Stroking dogs, using the sense of touch, can be immensely valuable, for young people who have been physically hurt or seen a loved one physically hurt, and have a restorative dimension, making them feel happy. It has been discovered from brain scans, that this can release the chemical oxytocin, from their brain, which is transferred into their bloodstream, causing them to have a happier state of mind. This is the opposite of serotonin, which is a chemical released in the brain of a person who has suffered or witnessed unpleasant abusive incidents, giving them a depressive feeling. Embracing a dog can also give a sense of warmth, and belonging to a young person.

A very famous Labrador called Endel changed his owner at a profound level, from being very depressed and withdrawn, through simply giving him love and attention. This led to him feeling happy again and restored his marriage and family life. It was observed that Endel would often look at the left hand side of his owner's face, to understand his emotions! Therefore some dogs can have a sense of empathy, which may be valuable for therapists comfortable with using animals as a way of helping young people.

How I used animal therapy as a part of my therapeutic practice:

The following case studies are narratives of how I used animals therapeutically, to impact the lives of traumatised young people.

CASE STUDY ONE: BELONGING

This happened with one young person, called Tim whom I was working with, who responded from a question about his early life, 'can we please not talk about this Martin'. Following this I introduced two dogs, which I had at the time, who were very good-natured, friendly, and related well with children, having a lot of energy! They were a collie cross, called Jessie (female) and a golden Labrador called Max (Male).

Initially I introduced Max only, and found that this young person quickly related to him, on a local sandy beach, engaging in fun chase games! This led to him talking about his own family pets on the way home, and then a traumatic car crash involving himself and his mother.

Tim lived with relatives initially before going into care. His mother was affected by drug abuse, and not able to look after him, and his natural father was in prison. He had felt strong rejection in life, and it was hoped our sessions as well as giving him the opportunity to talk, could also focus on raising his self-esteem.

Max seemed to facilitate a relaxed sense in the young person, who spoke of low moments which were like a black hole, and that he then thought of a bulldozer which would strongly push the feelings away, though he had to work very hard for them to go; he felt talking about his concerns, helped the bulldozer. He went on to explain that the low moments came when he was thinking about his mother, and that he last saw her on a school day, expressing that he felt anger and sadness. It felt like Max was an emotional cushion, which facilitated such openness from this young person.

Subsequently, at the beginning of the next session, Tim shared that things had been difficult with his mum, and he didn't wish to talk about it. However, he found it a great release, giving a lot of attention to Max, feeling very relaxed running along a local beach with him. He seemed much happier. However, I also observed how he threw a tennis ball for Max, with a very powerful level of force, releasing a lot of anger, which just missed my head! Following this experience with Max on the beach, whilst on the journey home, he expressed that he was very angry after seeing his mother (for contact), because he wanted to stay with her, but couldn't let her know this because, he felt, it would upset her too much. He added that he felt 'let down'. He was a parent child, with all the weight of responsibility, which this involved.

Therefore Tim was able to 'reach' a very deep level of pain within himself, in an early phase of our sessions, after interacting with Max and talking with myself, after having held down his real feelings whilst with his mother. The key aspect was that the right environmental conditions were created for this to happen. This was having an animal, which the young person could relate to, which could give unconditional love, accompanying myself, within a relaxed and dynamic atmosphere of space (the sandy beach). In this situation the young person was able to show both joy, and release more difficult feelings e.g. anger, safely.

His relatives following this session reported that his anger was lessening, even though he spoke of his mother not turning up for a contact session. He also expressed, to me, that what we talked about last week helped him a lot.

Tim in a further session, asked about Max immediately (he was not with us in this session) and later spoke of 'his class just not knowing what its like and why I feel alone'. He went on to speak again of feeling let down, and that most of his class have parents or someone who loves them. I wondered whether he was also really missing Max. His pain increased by his best friend no longer playing with him at school, explaining that this was upsetting and causing him to hit his head against something (self-harm).

I asked Tim, what upset him most about this situation with his best friend, and he said that his friend had not explained to him why he was no longer his friend. This could link with the difficulty of his mother not explaining to him why she couldn't care for him or put him first, or simply why she couldn't turn up for contact. I was asked by Tim to speak with his teacher, which I followed through to seek to find out why he wouldn't play with him. His teacher identified from talking with his friend that it was because he misinterpreted from his parents that needing to work harder at school meant not playing with my client. It was then clarified, by the teacher to his friend that working harder did not mean he shouldn't play with his friends, and also explained to the young person whom I worked with. He then realised this was not specifically about himself being rejected, and he felt much happier, with the friendship between them being restored. Therefore a therapeutic involvement i.e. contacting his school, at his request, can have positive benefits.

However, there was still a detachment from Tim, reflected like a disassociation from present reality, in our sessions. I was aware that he was very worried that he could no longer live with his relatives, who were moving abroad and could not take him with them, and was informed by his Social Worker, that he would need to be supported in a foster placement. I also felt there was a gap of pain, which he was not ready to share with me.

However, I was aware that he loved mountain biking, which I also enjoyed, and we decided to complete a local trail on rough ground, with Max coming too! Therefore animal therapy can link with outdoor development (previous section).

In the upward leg of the trail, he shared that he "felt like sleeping on his bike, and firing machine gun bullets out everywhere". It seemed valuable to him that he could express this, and I quietly reflected whether this linked to his desire to run away from a growing despair which he felt, and yet hit out at people and life where he had felt let down. Tim found the downhill leg exciting and dynamic, and asked in our next session, to return to this trail with our mountain bikes, and with Max.

Whilst we were preparing to ride in the following session, Tim was in a very positive frame of mind, and I asked him how he was feeling this week. He replied that things were better now with his friend, and they were playing a lot at school, which he felt very happy about. I then asked, whether he had been able to see his mother, which I was aware was very important to him, and he found it really difficult to answer. He suddenly looked at Max, who was next to him, as were preparing to go, and stroked him continually. Following this he said, "Max is my mum with boy". Although Max was a male dog, the young person saw him, in female gender, with his soft coat and warmth of expression. I felt he was releasing his sense of loss through Max, and was seeing in Max the love that he desired from his mother, and perhaps couldn't receive, and acceptance of him unconditionally. There was also the love, which he could show to Max, practically, through touch, which showed a depth of expression, as Max focused his eyes towards the young person, too moving for Tim to express.

The trail was over 2 miles of uphill and downhill ground and tough terrain, which the young person found rewarding to achieve. Max ran alongside us. On the return downward leg, which Tim found exhilarating, he felt a real sense of achievement. I gave him opportunity to share any concerns or anything special, and he responded that he was "worried about mum". I asked if he could say what the worry was, and he couldn't answer, and I quickly intervened that some things are too hard to put into words. He looked at Max, and agreed, and said to me, 'you do understand about what I am going through, but you cannot really know', which I felt was right

Following this, in further sessions Tim's processing developed, after sharing that he also felt isolated from his father. This was reflected through being able to focus on both happy and traumatic memories of him. He spoke of driving around fast in a scrap yard with his father, feeling very happy, and in contrast recalled his father 'going to hit him (he was at a young age), and his mother standing in the way, but she was hit in the nose and it was bleeding'. He went on to say, that he wouldn't have minded his dad hitting him, but not his mother.

It was the deepest memory of pain I felt Tim had spoken of, which I recognised could account for him feeling responsible for his mother, and possibly a guilt which may have impacted his self-esteem, and been a contributory factor causing anger both with himself, and towards his father. He went on to speak of feeling more pain from being unloved-even though his aunt and uncle showed this towards him as he could only see the absence of love from his mother and father—than even feeling let down, and that no one wanted to see him a lot. He felt, symbolically, he added, like he and his father were in his (Tim's) body, but that he was one side and his father was on the other side, and that his father was walking away from him, while someone in the middle was firing bullets at him. This seemed a powerful allegorical picture, which allowed him to reach much deeper levels of feeling and understanding. His father was in prison at the time. He didn't seem to know the person firing the bullets.

In a further session, I introduced both of our dogs. This seemed to fascinate Tim, and he quickly said that Jessie (female collie cross) was his dad, and Max (male Labrador) was his mum. Later in the session, I asked him if he could share more about Jessie being his dad, and he said that his dad had black hair, like Jessie, and she had her tongue out like his dad sometimes did. He went on to say, that Max had a woman's face, and blond hair, which his mother has, and he has a gentle look, which his mother was sometimes like. This seemed quite important comparative imagery, for this young person, as he had not been able before, to talk about both his parents at the same time, and never spontaneously. I felt it was restorative for him.

In the following session, he expressed his concern over his mother, as he had not seen her for contact, and that he was wondering how much his mother loved him. I empathised with this, and Tim felt able to talk very naturally, saying 'that the biggest gap, was not being able to be with his mother, and this was higher a gap than any feeling, although talking filled a big gap'. I felt this gave valuable feedback, not asked for, about the value of introducing animals in therapy, not only for the value of it within itself, as shown above, but that it can also facilitate the ability of the young person to build up the emotional resources to talk about the most painful aspects of his or her life. He asked if I could contact his Social Worker to see if his mother would meet him.

A few months later he spoke again of the value of talking, sharing that through talking with me the magnets (symbolic examples of his relationship with his parents) are constantly coming together, and coming apart slightly, and then coming back, as if this was normal in his emotional processing. I reflected in an intuitive sense, if this imagery may also represent, as well as his relationship with his parents, the child part of him connecting with the very young child (pre-trauma). This was through the process of therapeutic and all round support he was getting from school and social care. I reflected, from Tim's imagery, whether he was able to release the guilt and anger that he was feeling with himself, and towards his parents, and very gradually become more of a whole person, rather than fragmented, or frozen from the trauma of the time. In other words, that he was 'thawing out'. This may possibly be indicated by his comment that 'he could cope with the pressures of school in a more even keeled way now'.

Following the above expressions of loss, Tim spoke in the next session of finding things less painful in respect of his mother, through talking. He added that things were better at school and that he received a special award for good work, which was presented in assembly, and which he had not received in a long time, and that he felt "very proud". At the same time this young person also received strong support from Social Care, and his school, which he found positive. He also, in the following weeks, received more regular calls from his father, which he always spoke about when we met, and was encouraged. He felt like a connection was now taking place again with his father, described by him, 'as two magnets coming together, though which had not yet reached the point of magnetic connection'.

Max was present in these sessions, without specific mention being made concerning him, and during this time Tim referred back to the trauma when his father hit his mother. He shared that he was not responsible and yet, he added, he was. I intervened that as a child he could not help what happened, which he responded well to, saying that he previously felt it was his fault. He added that he felt like two magnets, had come a long way together, and was happier. It was interesting that he gave no indicator of who the second magnet related to, whether his father, Max or myself, or whether it related to two parts of himself, or himself and his mother! There was also a profound sense of symbolic mystery with this young person, though I wonder whether the second magnet related to his father.

In subsequent sessions, Tim was enjoying sand constructions in a beach environment, and although not intensively involved it seemed important that Max was present. He spoke of having little gaps within himself now, one for his mother, one for his father, and one for his best friend. He also referred to being able to cope with school better, and was keen, in a further session, to accompany me to take my two dogs to the vets for a routine check up. Whilst at the vets, where there was a quiet respectful atmosphere, he was prompted to recall his past again, saying that he didn't like being shouted at, at school, and in a separate reflection, that his step-father always shouted at him. He then suddenly, expressed, that he could now understand why he was so angry at being shouted at, at school, that it was due to his stepfather shouting. He was becoming more self-aware.

Tim also expressed that he was happy in his new foster placement, but missed his mother very much, and found it really difficult that someone older than himself had different –age appropriate boundaries to himself. There was a sense of unfairness emerging for this young person, in his perception, though it was encouraging that he could express his real feelings, and understandable to feel this difficulty of unfairness when he had felt, the carer for his mother. He was adjusting, though painful, to being cared for without having to feel responsible for his mother. I affirmed that this must be difficult for him, but expressed that he was a young person, and did not need to take that responsibility for his mother, which he listened to carefully.

In these final sessions, I did not always take Max, and there was a positive sense that this young person was building the emotional strength within himself, without the cushion of Max, being there. This was demonstrated by sessions on the beach in which he saw his friends playing football and was keen to join them, as a group activity, though happy for me to be present and join in, or watch. However, the key focus was his interaction with his friends. His foster carers stimulated his interest in football, and arranged for him to join a local team, which he really enjoyed and which helped him with his social interaction, and also fostered his self-esteem. This was really valuable.

Therefore, the involvement of animals, in helping him therapeutically, can have considerable impact when introduced, and the emotional affects of the interaction are fostered with the young person. When sensitively attuned to the young person their involvement, can then be lessened in time, according to his needs, as he draws increasingly from his own emotional resources. In the case of Tim, he was gaining strength through self-awareness and self-expression, alongside a stable foster placement, and positive peer group interaction.

This continued with him expressing his frustration with his father not contacting him, after coming out of prison, though it was encouraging that this was made explicit to me, rather than internalised as anger. This showed real personal growth. Tim expressed that he felt 'angry, sad and disappointed', and that he realised that this affected how he was with other children. He went on to share that his feeling of why has this happened to me i.e. not having a mum and dad to live with, and not other children (the sense of unfairness), was expressed by him by kicking other children. He made the connection himself without any support. He also felt that being aware that other people have difficulties too was helping, after which he added 'that he was ok with his mother now'.

In our final session, with Max present, Tim said, that he felt much happier now, confirmed by his foster carers too, and that his father speaks with him on the phone now, which meant a lot to him. He was very settled in his placement, and looking forward to going to his new school, and again used symbolism sharing that the magnets were touching closely with his father, and overlapping. This was a positive outcome from a very traumatic phase in his childhood, in which Max and Jessie were vital cushions of feeling and expression for Tim, to allow him to move forwards in his life.

In conclusion, to this case study it may be possible to formulate a 'model of affect' from using animals in therapeutic work (below). This has a simple but profound affect using the above case study as a template.

MODEL OF AFFECT

Stage one: Introducing the animals to build trust, and engagement e.g. Max playing on the beach with the young person.

Stage two: Allowing the child to identify with the animals e.g. the child stroking Max, and looking at him.

Stage Three: Release of traumatic pain through sensory interaction (e.g. sight, touch)

Stage Four: Providing (from stage 3) the emotional resources for the young person to talk about painful areas and release painful feelings, with the therapist, or someone he trusts.

Stage Five: Understanding from the child that it is not their fault.

Stage six: Integrating more fully into their school and home life (with family or in care).

CASE STUDY TWO: UNDERSTANDING

It will be interesting to examine, if this model of approach matches the process, which the following young person, called Richard went through, whom I worked with, using Max and Jessie. This is an in-depth narrative. He has special needs.

Richard was referred to me through Social Care, as someone showing complex and serious emotional problems, having difficulties settling at home and in specialist schools. It was proving very difficult to find him a school placement. He was described as having strong autistic traits, or 'having autism', and was referred to a child psychiatrist (which I attended), during the early phase of our sessions, to seek to understand if he had any awareness of his behaviour affecting other people, both children and adults. His family and social care had explained that he also had strong anger issues, and difficulty with social skills, as well as finding it very difficult to cope with lots of people around him. His attention span was very short. However, it was felt a longer period of time could be beneficial for this young person, for each session, as it was very hard for him to develop trust.

At an introductory meeting I met Richard with his mother and Social Worker, and it emerged that he was very interested in animals. We all agreed it would be a sensitive introduction, for me to take him to visit a local tropical bird centre. The young person was very settled and showed a lot of patient interest in the different species of birds, recollecting that he had been there once before with his family. He was also particularly attracted to the guinea pigs and rabbits, and liked their soft coats. Following this, he asked to see the farm animals, particularly the goats, whose appearance and behaviour he liked.

At this point, he felt confident enough to express his thoughts, and shared that it was really important to treat animals with care and respect, and then talked about his own experiences in a specialist school, which he had previously attended. Richard was appreciative of our first session (5.5hrs), and twice thanked me for the birds and animals, which he saw.

In our next session, I met Richard at his home, and was introduced to his family. The young person also had other interests as well as animals, which he felt secure in, expressing that his favourite activity was crazy golf. He reacted very positively to my suggestion to engage in this activity, and enjoyed playing in a local crazy golf course. He showed confidence returning to this same activity after his lunch break, and showed a very good attention span. After initial fear at "not being laughed at", he went on to play the game with increasing confidence, even though there were many members of the public around. He also had to wait his turn on a number of occasions, and showed a lot of patience. His skill level improved as he relaxed more.

During the lunch break, I asked him about any friends from his previous school, which he spoke of in our first session, and he found it very difficult to answer, being very reluctant to engage about this aspect of his life. There was a clear indicator of avoidance, and then a sharp contrast when I changed the conversation to my dogs, which he seemed very interested to meet, remembering that they were called Max and Jessie.

Afterwards I suggested cycling as a second outdoor activity, for the session, and after initial caution about the size of the bike he would have to ride, the young person enjoyed the experience, really appreciating the breeze. However, after a pause to rest he suddenly asked to stop, and return, though still very happy. The whole session was for 5 hrs.

I felt he was certainly building up self-confidence, and trust with myself, through outdoor activities, and a focus on animals (stage one of the above model).

Just before our next session, I was informed by Social Care, that Richard had to leave his home, and that he could naturally be very affected by this. However, he reacted well to an outdoor visit to a steam train centre, and particularly playing crazy golf. He was building safe areas of enjoyment and achievement i.e. skills/interests which he knew he could achieve or enjoy, and again referred to having previously been to this centre with his family. He asked me, in a moving way, whist we were on the train ride, what was going to happen to him, and where was he going to go at the end of the day. It was a huge emotional shock for him, in coming to terms with having to leave his home. I was impacted 'within' myself, and felt a real sense of, how can this young person really be answered in a way which he can make any sense of, or accept easily. At this point I noticed that he moved in an uncharacteristic way, into a deeper depressive sense, as in disassociation, where there was no communication from him. He stared at the steam ahead, looking completely pre-occupied.

At this point I intervened, referring him back to the steam journey, which he reacted well to. The young person followed the same structure as before, enjoying crazy golf in the morning, a lunch break eating the same food, of a pasty and chips, and then a return to Crazy golf in the afternoon. The sense of order seemed to help him. He was able to improve his skills as he relaxed further in this activity, responding well to encouragement.

Following this he asked to go on the steam train again, which he really enjoyed, sharing a carriage with a young mother and her children. He was incredibly well settled as he looked at them, and immediately asked me questions about my two dogs, and was very keen to meet them in our next session, in the same week. He then suddenly recalled, where he was going at the end of the day, speaking about his foster dad, who had a field, which he pointed out to me on the journey home to the children's centre. He referred to a horse in the field, which he really liked. This prompted him to speak spontaneously about some dogs which he had happy memories of, and that his first dad had a farm which he really enjoyed being on. As I said goodbye to him, at the end of our session, there was a lot of concern expressed in his eyes about where he was going to stay, as he looked back towards me. This session was also for 5 hrs, which became the norm in all our sessions.

In our next session, I introduced Max and Jessie to him. He really enjoyed seeing them, and gave them a lot of attention. We visited a locality, which I knew well, for exercising dogs, with a large field used by members of the public. Richard built up a good rapport with Max, throwing the ball for him, and quickly said, that Max was his second best friend. After this we went to a nearby beach, and had a pastie and chips for lunch, with both of us sitting alongside each other. This was very important for this young person who didn't wish me to sit opposite him.

He was then keen to visit seals and other marine creatures at a sea sanctuary, and remembered that he had also been there before with his family. He recalled that he most enjoyed the seals looking at him, in the underwater section. When we arrived, I spoke of keeping the windows down for our two dogs, to have enough air, after which he spoke of the importance of giving them, plenty of water to drink too. I asked him to take responsibility for this, and he then gave both the dogs some water, which he took very seriously. There was a real sense of care and responsibility being shown.

Richard asked to go straight to the underwater section of the seal sanctuary, and seemed to have very happy memories of that visit, recalling how much he liked the seals swimming to the glass and staring straight at him. There seemed a special bond for him, as he did this again, staring back at the seals, which seemed to give him a lot of pleasure (stage 2). This was in real contrast to his reactions to people staring straight at him! It was also interesting seeing that the official talk or feeding time had no interest for him, and which he didn't wish to watch.

Following this, he asked to go into the play area, and in a moment of uncertainty cried out 'help me mum', which he had intuitively done before on a couple of occasions with other activities. He was enjoying the swings and balancing apparatus, and there was a part of him, who recognised his age, saying 'lets pretend I am a baby', and another part, which had a real need to experience this aspect of play to fulfil a deeper, need. It seemed like he wished for a part of his early childhood to be restored, as the tone of his cry, 'help me mum', suggested something like a childhood trauma, where he quickly needed his mother in some way. This may be a clue to the strong anger, which he was showing at present, though he is also unable to live with his family now, and is in residential care. He had most enjoyed a sensory connection with the seals, and the play apparatus, though moved very quickly for his age through the rest of the sanctuary, like a young child, and suddenly said 'lets go now'. He spoke of wishing to take out the two dogs again, and was concerned for their welfare.

The significance for him of interaction with animals continued, and this was accompanied by less emotional distress, and more focus on activities, such as mini golf, which he could succeed in for longer periods of time.

This was encouraging, and in follow up sessions he would constantly interact with Max, whilst sitting on a beach, where touch was really important to him. The modification, which I had to introduce, was to help him to avoid putting pressure on Max to stay close to him, through pulling gently at him, and instead allowing Max to be himself and come to him in his own time. This may relate to a much deeper need to have a secure attachment, or a more nurturing warmth of relationship, from an early age, and being near an affectionate animal such as Max was possibly a way of fulfilling this.

Richard also felt very secure, if we sat on a small blanket, which had clear perimeters to it in which he would always ask for myself, and Max, to be sat within the blanket and not on the edges. If Max was on the edge, for example, he would be very concerned for him to sit much closer to the middle, and this would be his main focus (stage two).

Therefore, I reflected whether as well as his additional needs, or what was considered to be autistic traits, there was also a deeper need for a close attachment, and nurturing process, reflected in his attitude towards animals, and particularly related to Max. Perhaps this was filling a deeper childhood gap or need, in a profound way for him, and also symbolised the importance of belonging to him (stage 3).

At the same time he was able to focus on tasks more easily than before, or catch up slowly on his chronological age emotionally and cognitively e.g. less immediacy in suddenly throwing down a gold club, if upset beforehand, and stopping the activity in an angry manner.

However, there were challenging situations in his care placement, where staff were concerned that he was not responding to boundaries. Nevertheless, within our sessions, alongside an emerging anger in the young person (he may have been missing his home too), there was a positive sensory interaction with Max (stage 3). I also introduced Jessie, our collie cross. This delighted Richard who referred to them constantly, asking when he could take them for a walk and throw the ball for them. This positive sense of engagement, with both dogs, seemed to facilitate, an openness to talk about his family more sharing that he was looking forward to seeing his brother for the weekend. He was also interested in someone suffering from Parkinson's disease, whom I knew, asking how he was getting on.

There was therefore, as he became more secure, a process of more awareness of other people beyond himself, which was a step towards understanding the affect of his behaviour on other people. The interaction with both dogs seemed to foster this process, in terms of facilitating a positive state of mind within him. The pleasure for Richard too, in seeing Max catch a ball, which he had thrown, which was a one ness of interaction, of cause and affect, was immense. An action, which he created i.e., throwing a ball, was matched by the response of someone else, to his action i.e. Max catching the ball. The key aspect was that the interaction was mutually positive, and both the young person's needs and Max's was fulfilled, as a team. It is also interesting Max was impacting him more than Jessie (our collie-Cross), although he always spoke of the two dogs together.

At the same time staff at the short term residential centre, spoke of this young person beginning to talk now about past issues. Richard, in our following session (7hrs), asked to engage in a new activity, playing pool, which we followed through in a local hotel while Max, waited in the car. However, he seemed to be taking a long time to play each stroke, as if his mind was somewhere else, which was a new pattern of behaviour in our sessions. I was aware that there was a deeper issue affecting him.

I then suggested that we could go to a local garden centre, to buy Max a special ball, which he could then throw, which animated the young person. I asked him to choose the ball he wanted to throw for Max, along with four dog treats, which seemed empowering for him. This really motivated him, and on the way back, he expressed suddenly that 'when he was 7 a lady called Joan threatened him with a knife, and his brother had to defend him, before they ran away 3 miles back to their home, and that this was very frightening. He was also very precise sharing that this lady "treated him badly" (stage 4). Following this expression, and a further session of pool where he outworked further anger, reflected by playing shots frequently without waiting for my turn, the young person relaxed, as if a pressure lid had been lifted off him, and afterwards was skipping along with Max.

I encouraged him to talk further with people whom he felt he could trust, such as the staff at his centre, and he responded "like Max". There was therefore a huge bond of trust between them, reflected with a long hug, which he gave Max before returning to his residential care centre.

This developed as Max and I, were then asked by staff, to support Richard alongside them in the transition to settling down for the night. This was becoming increasingly challenging for them, as the young person who had autistic tendencies, was becoming very agitated with visual images of creatures attacking him, in his mind. A key aspect in this support, was the telling of imaginary stories, of the adventures of Max and Jessie-which had a reality to them which Richard found harmless and fun. This allowed him to settle, during night periods, and was for a one-hour period at the end of our sessions. It was interesting to hear the insights of other professionals in residential care, who felt that Max and Jessie provided security and continuity for the young person which was crucial for him, when he faced an uncertain future, in his own mind.

This allowed him to speak of further traumatic incidents from his past, precipitated by agitated behaviour and the coughing up of phlem, in our sessions. This included a huge family row between his older sister and father during a recent Christmas, which frightened him, and further references to the lady who attacked him with a knife, who he said was very kind to her own children but horrible to himself and his brother, giving them horrible food to eat. Following being able to make this explicit the young person calmed very quickly, asking to take the dogs for a walk and look after them. There was a restorative aspect to animal therapy therefore, which then allowed Richard to re-focus on aspects of learning, and awareness of the needs of others.

This was reflected in his ability to ask questions about the types of ships visiting a port, counting them, for example, and settle to some textbook work on animals and language i.e. re-arrangement of letters, which were not remotely possible in our early sessions. This could be a preparation for a return to a suitable school placement. He would also ask after other children whom I worked with, and how my day had gone before we met. This emerged through routine structure, which he could assimilate to reduce any anxiety, and then have the capacity to process awareness of others beyond him self. An emerging signal of this was sitting on the same picnic mat with us, eating a pastie and chips, and looking out on harmless scenes of people on the beach and ships in the distance, asking questions when intrigued, though also silently watching, in a very calm way.

Therefore, a special animal to a young person, showing warmth and affection, can provide a secure attachment, which he may not have had from his primary attachment figure, usually his mother, as a young child, or which he may have had but which was damaged by a traumatic incident. This can then restore an absence or gap in his development, or nurturing, which he may have been seeking all his life, but not been able to express or explain, but which had led to behaviour patterns either ambivalent or avoidant from him, causing a disruption both emotionally and cognitively, affecting both his home and school life. In addition to have this compounded by autistic ingredients, may make life feel very frightening and insecure, for such a young person whom I was working with. It can only make absolute sense, coming from this background, for him to find significance in someone e.g. Max, who can both give and receive love, as a young child would need. Richard's parents were very supportive and simply needed support to help and understand him. They also found that they could not cope for long periods with him staying at home.

The key underlying aspect in all the sessions, which were for 5-6 hrs (twice a week) for a six month period, was having a secure attachment with Max and myself, and a clear routine alongside this. This precipitated the opportunity for personal development for Richard to build from this security (including staff from his residential support centres who were vital to him) to try out new places and people to meet, with a new self-confidence.

This emerged with the local authority providing an opportunity to visit a specialist centre, with new staff, to support social interaction, and skill development, for this young person where there would be new adults present, and other young people. However, the emphasis was still on one to one support at this stage. This transitional stage was developed with myself being present with familiar staff from Richard's residential centre, at the outset of the session, usually for about one hour, and then leaving the young person when he felt secure, to get Max, and return with him (after 2 hrs), to meet Richard, and then continue our routine as we did beforehand. This worked very effectively, and prepared the way for him to go to a new residential school placement, appropriate for his needs.

However, on one occasion, I was aware of internal anxieties within Richard, when meeting him at the specialist centre, which may have related to his past trauma of abandonment as a young child, and which would be compounded by another change to a new school. After offering to take him with me to meet Max after half an hour, rather than his usually routine, it was felt by staff that he would be ok without this intervention. However, an hour after leaving he erupted into a very strong level of anger, which left staff shocked and shaken, and needing further support from members of staff from his care setting. I was contacted to return immediately with Max. As I approached the centre, I felt, the level of tension involved, and let Max quietly enter. The change was profound in which Richard reacted with joy, and hugged him, immediately calming, and returning to normal behaviour for the rest of the day. The attachment was vital for him, and shows even with a secure process of change, complexities emerge.

He shared afterwards, in our session, that he was so angry because he was worried about Max. This could have related to his concerns for him, after he leaves the locality, and although he knew he was well cared for, the importance of this attachment, and the level of interaction involved, may have been very hard to let go of, and triggered by Max's absence (even though part of his routine) on this specific occasion. I recall the look on the young persons face, as Max returned to him, changing with such immediacy, and how restorative this was.

This led to Richard focusing on further new challenges and activities, which he himself wanted to overcome. This included visiting a well known castle which as well as having an educational interest for him, and preparing him for school, had darker shaded rooms, which he felt a fear of, linked to his past, and visions of imaginary creatures appearing, but which he himself said "I must overcome this". He asked for Max and myself, to be alongside him, and from this entered such rooms in the castle, and underground public passages, and felt very pleased that he had overcome this fear, which had not been possible before. He was fascinated by the second world war food of the soldiers. A further major challenge was large crowds of people, which with his autistic traits was very hard to cope with. However, on Max's birthday, he insisted on going into a crowded shop and buying him a present, and with support to focus on this, rather than the people around him he succeeded, and felt proud of himself. This was also preparation for school.

A creative awareness from a therapist, working with animals, can also utilise other situations for young people with additional needs, to overcome cognitive and emotional challenges. One further example was when I had to take Max to the vets, for an injection. Max was very nervous, and I asked Richard if he wanted to come too. Even though he found it hard to visit formalised centres, he shared 'I feel this is hard, but I must go in'. When following this through, he came with me into the consulting room, met the vet, and quietly calmed Max very effectively, and achieved further progress in social confidence.

The awareness of Richard of soon having to leave his family and friends-to go to his new residential school-, although hard, was important, in allowing a natural grieving process to take place, regarding his attachment to Max, and a positive sense of letting go. On one occasion, in one of our concluding sessions, he suddenly asked if we could stop, in a pub car park, which had a lot of grass next to it. We got out, and he sat down in front of the car. He explained to me, that he wanted to spend extra time talking to Max, and gave him some very strong hugs, which were not aggressive in any way, but were empathising, almost like a sense of loss. I had not felt this level of feeling within him before (stage 5). I felt he was saying goodbye in his own way and was in control of this, in an empowering sense, which I felt was both therapeutic and restoring because of the suddenness of leaving his previous school, and even his home. This had been out of his control.

Alongside this, his sense of care for Max throughout all our sessions was excellent, always providing water, giving food when we felt appropriate, opening windows to give adequate ventilation for him, and recreational fun with a ball thrower, along with affection when on the picnic mat. This was perhaps a picture of what he himself feels is so important to give to others, and in return only wishing for acceptance and love, which Max gave naturally. His family, very much sought to fulfil this for him, and he was always very keen to return home for visits.

Following this special goodbye, although Max was still very important to him, by simply being present, he was not the key focus. Richard suggested that he and I both play badminton on the pub lawn. He mentioned that he used to play this game and felt he was quite good at it. He had good co-ordination, and I felt normality in his behaviour beginning to come through. He then suddenly said, 'could you do some school work with me', taking out some English worksheets, which even two weeks ago he had dismissed angrily, when they were given to me by his mother'. This was a remarkable change, and was part of the above process, which led to him adapting successfully to a new residential school placement (stage 6).

I was involved in taking him up to this school initially and back home for holidays, to maintain continuity, and in our last three sessions, although touch contact with Max was very important still, -on the picnic rug-, his focus now was more on other drama or sport activities. He was also able to be more self-aware, sharing that he realised that a film of someone attacking someone else frightened him so much because his brother was threatened by a group of boys near where he lived, recently. To my understanding Richard has continued to settle in residential education centres, and is doing well.

Therefore, animal therapy can play a rewarding role, in restoring traumatic attachment difficulties which young people have, even with complex special needs, and feelings which may not easily be apparent but which are as profound and deep as any one else's. It certainly allowed Richard to move forward in his life.

CASE STUDY THREE: EXPRESSION

The following case study involved a young person, called Mark who had witnessed severe physical abuse between his parents, and his mother affected with alcoholism (during the time of our sessions she was no longer affected by alcohol). While this happened he became mute at the age of 6, and was in need of therapeutic support. Our sessions began when Mark was aged 7. He was originally living with his father and grandmother, along with the rest of his family, though later in our sessions, lived with his mother. It was felt that Mark was caught in the middle of an ongoing conflict between his parents who were separated, and could find it very difficult to talk about this. This proved to be the case, and therefore I introduced Jessie to Mark, as part of our sessions (both parents were very supportive of our sessions).

As I introduced Jessie (our Labrador Max was engaged with other young people), I found that Mark could relax and enjoy taking Jessie along a local beach, and throw the ball for her, which she ran to collect (stage one). This led to him enjoying other activities in the local sand park, building his self-confidence through climbing, balancing, and sliding. He made very good choices about which activity to pursue and was also very keen on football. There was a sense of security that Jessie provided for Mark which allowed him to be himself and share, his feelings about his father, and his concerns for his mother's well being. He also felt able to share his challenges at school. When there was a session where I couldn't bring Jessie (often in very hot conditions), Mark would ask where she was, with a real sense of absence.

In responding to this and bringing her in the following session (weather conditions were ok) he felt very happy and suddenly said, "mum was drunk and now she is better", and this made me feel "sad", and that after she stopped and I felt "happy". He was able to reach his deeper feelings, which had not been possible before, or even speak at any level when 6. I supported this openness, sharing that your mother although drunk still would have had a love for you, which he reacted well to, and also that 'because you were small you could not be expected to have helped your mother', which he also seemed relieved to hear, adding 'the second smallest' (he had a younger brother)!

It is possible that this engagement with Mark could have happened without Jessie, or any animals being present, though factually, there was a real difference in his ability to 'be himself' through Jessie being present, almost having a normalising affect on Mark perhaps. He also responded well to expressing his feelings through drawings at the end of each session, which included Jessie chasing an "alien alligator away" (stage two). There may have been a sense of empowerment, which Mark gained from Jessie, reflected in what he could express about his mother and in his drawings, which may link with the spontaneous play reactions with Jessie on the sandy beach.

The use of height and dynamic activity such as swings was also important for Mark, in overlooking the landscape, and as he looked up to the sky he spoke of seeing the clouds and heaven, and then that he saw me up in the sky with a bird, though a little later thought it was Jessie.

He continued to progress in self-confidence in both football skills, where he was keen to express tackling and shoulder charges, and in the park apparatus. His father also spoke very positively of him having a really good end of year report from school. At the same time, there was a sensory engagement from Mark where he would see small pools of water on the plastic surface cover of a boat, describing them as lakes between high mountains, suggesting that we spray each of our pools of water onto the other parts of the plastic together. This could also be seen as Mark being strengthened through being himself, represented by the lakes of water and then able to overcome the mountain of being silent in his life; Mark had also been able to express his desire to his father to see his mother for contact, which was empowering for him.

Tragically during this phase of our sessions Jessie died, whilst at home with my son, and I was looking for the right opportunity to share this with Mark, who became close to her. When Jessie had been absent when ill, Mark had asked about her, and also his mother. This was also a sensitive time, for Mark, with his mother and father no longer together, and his grandmother in hospital. Alongside this, his mother was looking for him to change primary schools (for sound practical reasons), which would involve loss of friends initially.

However, Mark had again found it strengthening to look from the highest point of the play park, where he gained a sense of perspective, speaking with animation of the rocks out in the sea, which he could see. I felt this was his way of rising above his family circumstances, and sadness. Therefore as I was standing on the rampart of the play park with him looking out to sea, I let him know that Jessie had died. There was a real sadness in his eyes, though also resilience, and he asked me 'how did she die'. I responded that it was older age, which was correct, though I also quietly knew that she had been affected by the sad loss of Max who died just two months before. Mark looked at me, and said 'that she was in heaven in a better place now where no one could be unkind to her, and a spaceship could go up to her and bring her down to the rest of us, with other people who were up there too'. He seemed strengthened that I had shared this with him, along with his sadness (stage two). Following this, we had a fun race back to the car, before he returned to his mother.

In our next session, Mark was keen to show me his drawings of seals from a seal sanctuary, which he had visited, showing he said, a large seal and then baby seals poorly in hospital, which he clearly felt for. There was a growing compassion and link with animals suffering coming through.

During this session, I could also see his growing self-confidence through climbing down plastic ropes, for example, which he had not been able to do before, and expressing himself in sand art pictures, in which he drew his brother whom he is very close to. However, I sensed that Mark was not really focused this session, which had not happened before, and asked him 'how he was feeling', to which he said, 'I'm not sure and can't think about feelings'.

I felt this connected with sadness, and shock, over the loss of Jessie, and spoke of the positive time we had with her, which he seemed to relate to very quickly. He asked to go near a small shop, in the village, though his mind seemed elsewhere, and he didn't wish to go in, without being able to express anything. I then intervened with a special moment from a past session, when, Mark ran towards a dog which he thought was Jessie, nearby, and it wasn't, and it prompted him to say in this session, 'she was down there by the gate in the opposite direction to where I thought'.

We then both went down to the field where she ran in our sessions, as I knew Mark had been very concerned for her, and he suddenly said "lets have it quiet now" (stage three), which was by the fence where he chased to, to try to get her back. This was a remarkable thing to say, and I felt it allowed Mark to connect with thinking about Jessie at this time, rather than this being minimised (stage three). Following this he seemed to feel much better, and said 'lets have another chase game'. This involved a race back to the car!

We were therefore engaged in a grieving process, which Mark was feeling, and which I had gone through, which I felt was important not to push away, for fear of upsetting him further. After this Mark asked to look around the shop he originally wished to go to, which he then enjoyed. We returned to his mother, who spoke of Mark previously being angry and hitting her, and after calming down being able to say that he didn't wish to be like that. However, she went on to say, that after I spoke to him about Jessie's passing in our previous session, she was encouraged because he was able to be so open about the sadness which he felt about Jessie, and even though he was very upset and cross with his mum, there was no aggression. He also allowed her to help him, and she spoke of Jessie being with his grandfather in heaven now, and in a much better place', which he responded well to. This process with Jessie, although completely unforeseen, allowed Mark to have opportunity to grieve, and identify with his sadness with his grandfather's passing, though also significantly allowed his relationship with his mother to grow as they talked together about loss. This was a very positive development (stage four).

It also prepared Mark for the future loss of his paternal grandmother, whom I met on a number of occasions, and whom Mark was devoted to. It was a complete shock to him, and happened suddenly while she was away. It was very hard for Mark's father who was suffering from this sad loss him self, to see the loss, which Mark too was feeling, and this was the pressure and sadness, which Mark was carrying within himself i.e. he was suffering too but felt his dad didn't realise this. His mother was very aware of this, and yet it was hard for Mark to express this to his father.

At the same time however, I had a new young Golden Labrador called Lionel (18months old), whom I was introducing to children. He had gone through a very traumatic background himself, and was nervous of older women and some men with hoodies, though I felt he might be able to connect powerfully with traumatised children, and identify with them. This was an unknown process, which I felt was worth pursuing (in contrast to Max and Jessie who were very affectionate and welcomed attention from all adults, children and young people), after realising that he reacted well to making initiatives himself, rather than having people come to him, which caused him to run away. This led to situations outdoors where he became completely opposite to his initial behaviour pattern, lost his fear of people and loved engaging with children and young people with fun antics on the beach involving a ball being thrown and then running to catch it. The key was to explain to the young person, that they should do the opposite to chasing, and allow Lionel to come to them. This worked, and Lionel engaged powerfully with Mark, who was very receptive.

Mark was delighted to play with Lionel, throwing the ball for him to collect, and laughing a lot. However, I observed that he became very angry at a seagull nearby, shouting very loudly, for him to go away as the seagull was scavenging to take something away. I felt this was a powerful symbolic picture or trigger of loss for Mark-something being taken away, which was near him and expressed well beyond normal irritation. There was anger within him, much stronger than what I had seen before, and following seeing the seagull, he asked to throw sand in my eyes and that we should both be power rangers and fight each other. I guided him away from fighting aggression, to a competitive race to the tide edge, which he reacted well to along with Lionel joining us in the race! However, it was fascinating that when we reached the sea, Mark wished to keep me on the sea-side, to gain a sense of control.

I was very aware how Mark had experienced considerable loss in his young life already, relating to the loss of family togetherness, which he longed to return, the sadness at how his mother and father were affected in their relationship, and the loss of his paternal grandfather, and now grandmother, alongside a new school and loss of old friends. Through all this Mark could do nothing to change events or bring these people back to life or together again, so that everyone would be happy. This was his real heart. There was even the challenge of what happened to Jessie, and this highlights that there can also be an emotional cost in animal therapy, alongside benefits, both to the young person, and to the therapist or helper! Therefore I could see where he was coming from. He was feeling completely helpless, along with feeling guilt.

Mark then asked for me, as a power ranger, to go out into the shallow sea and stay there for 10 minutes, and I quickly took off my shoes and socks, and felt it was important to run with these feelings. I encouraged him to give me a signal when he was ready for me to come in. We both agreed that the other power ranger Mark would not get his feet wet and could move backwards slowly as the tide came in, whereas the tide slowly became higher as I stayed in a stationary position (this was only up to my knees). This was taken very seriously by Mark, and I felt this was a necessary process for him, to release the level of complete helplessness, which he had always felt in his life, recognising that his strong anger was not directed to me, but towards the tragic circumstances of his life. Lionel was looking quite intrigued at this point, wondering what I was doing standing in rising sea-water!

After what was nearly 10 minutes, Mark gave a smile and said 'come in'. I was aware that his face seemed to lessen considerably in tension at this point, his aggression disappeared, and he returned to his normal self (stage 5), letting go of his own guilt.

This led to Mark feeling much more empowered in future sessions, and although there was challenges when living with his mother concerning having time and attention with his father, who had a new partner now and baby, there was a desire from both parents to do the best for Mark. Mark was now able to express his feelings much more immediately, and verbally now, and was keen for us both to go into the sea together now, after a fun session with Lionel on the beach. He was keen to go as far as he could in to the sea (relating to his need for clear boundaries), and I placed a boundary of only going as far as we could up to our knees which, he responded very well to. He also found it a lot of fun jumping the waves with me, as we stood side by side facing each wave. Mark was very relaxed and went on to say, that it was best when I was caught by a wave! He also expressed that "being in the sea was helping his angry and sad feelings to go away, and his happy feelings to stay". Lionel also joined us and stood facing some of the gentler waves! Therefore, the role of animals was at a supportive stage now, as Mark was gaining the necessary emotional strength to release his most painful feelings, without a deep engagement with Lionel. This was the same pattern as the above two case studies, involving Max.

He went on in our concluding sessions, to be able to respond to direct verbal questions from me, of a deeper nature. I asked him, 'how he was feeling now with his Nan's passing?' and he said I miss her very much and that I would like to see her each day in heaven. Mark had not spoken in such depth of feeling before, about a loss in his family.

Mark continued to engage well with Lionel, and was delighted when he offered Lionel some dog biscuits, and he took them from him. This was the first time he had taken them from another person. Mark gave a huge smile, and said, 'I am the best with him'. There were continuing challenges with Mark wanting to see more of his dad, as he was living with his mother now, though it was encouraging that Mark and his mum were now able to talk together about deeper issues affecting him. His mother was able to really support Mark effectively, concerning his father's withdrawal through his own grief, sharing that it wasn't about him, to avoid him being affected with rejection. This really helped Mark. Mark also spoke very enthusiastically about soon being able to have a puppy Labrador, of his own at home!

In his new school, after the summer holidays Mark continued to have challenges with change, both with his new school and friendships, sharing that he felt upset leaving his old school. He had also transferred his anger to the puppy who he was throwing around when upset, and said to his mum to take him away as he didn't wish to hurt him'.

However, Mark was also able to write in our session, "I am sad because Nanny has gone", and also spoke this out, which seemed to really help him, along with drawing a picture of how he felt. He pointed to the picture and the word sad particularly. I felt Mark was engaging very well now, which could help him in releasing the deeper level of anger, which he felt. He also found it releasing simply looking at the sea in this session, and at boats in the harbour, and suddenly said to me "dad said you are a good man".

Mark's continuing challenge were the symptoms of the deeper unfairness of life on himself. He spoke in a further session of bringing in his very special pencil case to his new school, given to him by his Nan before she died, and not getting a chance to talk about it, and that a child said it was only an ordinary pencil case, and that both these things made him feel angry and sad.

However, he was now able to express how he felt and also understand why he felt as he did more. He also showed ability to think how he could modify his own behaviour, sharing that having a buddy friend at his new school would help him to be less angry at home. He was happy for me to mention this to his mother, who then spoke to the school about how urgent this, was. I also gave strategies to Mark, including only talking to close friends whom he knew well very, and trusted, about very special things to him. He reacted well to this, and named his new school friends to me, as well as asking to draw a picture of Lionel, asking him 'to be good because you're special'.

Mark continued to express his anger at his Nan's passing-it was completely sudden while she was away and I supported this sharing it was fine to be angry because it showed how much he loved her, and that there were ways to show anger which were ok, such as drawing which Mark did. He also said, 'I write', which I affirmed.

Following this, Mark was happier at school with more friends, and integrating much better, as well as feeling settled at home, and having a choice when he went to see his dad. Mark spoke of not hitting out at home any more, and that the pain was getting slowly better with missing his Nan. His mother since the passing of Jessie was able to share more difficult issues with Mark, which helped him, and he was able to bring up that we had two more sessions only left, and that he would like to keep his drawing book to remember our time together. There was a positive acceptance of our ending, which was very encouraging. At the same time the role of Lionel was gradually lessened.

In our penultimate session, Mark identified that the painful parts left in him, were missing his grandma and granddad -a real development for him-, and with sensitive support, he remembered a happy memory of her smiling when he told a funny joke on his birthday. We spoke of how alongside sadness there are happy memories, which will never leave him. He reacted well to this, and was able to draw his Nan and granddad by the sea. He also wrote an allegorical message about them both, "the car is moving on the deep road in the sky", with a drawing of someone smiling in the car, which was a watermelon car. This was very restoring for him, after which he wrote a special poem about his Nan and granddad in the sky, sharing that the light was beautiful in the sky, which he sang to his mother at the end of our session. She was very moved, and it was encouraging that he wanted his mother to be very much a part of his sharing of grief, for the future (stage 6).

In our last session, there was a growing sense of adjustment in his new school, with positive new friendships emerging, alongside guidance how to relate to harsher comments. Mark also was able to highlight a happy memory with his grandfather, in which he was in his car and saw a wave come over the sea wall and into their car. This was encouraging. There was a very normal and accepting reaction from Mark to the ending of our sessions, including playing air hockey, and the gift of a lunch box (his suggestion!) to remember our time together with the dogs, when he goes into school (stage 6). There was a sense of sadness too, as Mark lingered for a short time, not wishing to let go of my car, but the lunch box conveyed a movement forwards for him after he received this, and from that moment he could let go completely. His mother at the same time, spoke of seeing a lot of changes in Mark, through our sessions, and mentioned the significance of Jessie and Lionel to him, in this process. She thanked 'the three of us' for what we had done!

Thematic Understanding:

There were other individualised benefits of animal therapy, which touched the lives of other young people whom I worked with. There follows 5 shorter themed examples, all of which involved children who had complex needs, whom I used my dogs for part of their therapeutic intervention. The emphasis was on allowing the young person to engage with the animals in a way which was natural for them, to allow them to find their point of need through this, and then having the opportunity to express it, either symbolically, or in a sensory way, or verbally. If sensitively supported by the therapist or helper, they can then understand this need, and the therapist can allow the animals to help restore the theme missing from the child's life. This can then help them to re-integrate into normal life e.g. in the case of Mark (above) the ability to be able to grieve, and be heard, allowed him to accept his mother's authority, and adapt to changes in going to a new school. This is the process of the six stages (above), or model of change.

Friendships

One young person called Peter, had suffered severe neglect in his life, and felt responsible for looking after his younger brothers. He also felt a sense of shock being removed from his birth family, and being taken into care, where it was very painful to begin to recognise that all he had accepted from his parents as being ok, was very different to the lifestyle he was leading with his foster carers. There was a sense of conflict for him where he wished to remain loyal to his birth family, but also became very angry at how he felt treated by them. This previous lifestyle led to him finding social relationships with his peers very difficult in secondary education, and also a gap between his chronological age and his emotional and cognitive levels. He was functioning at a younger age. It was hard for him to know ways of speaking, and appropriate boundaries, and through this he became very isolated.

On one occasion, Peter, who had made considerable progress in understanding his life and how he was affected by it in our sessions, along with strong support, from his foster family, and social care, wished to make positive friendships. He found it very hard to achieve this. One approach, which I used, was to allow him a sense of space, to be himself, and meet some school peers in the local play park (for a part of our session), which he asked to do. This was after school. I agreed with him that I would stay nearby with Lionel. This led to Peter slowly building up an engagement with the same group of young people over a period of weeks. This developed from a few minutes, to half an hour, with Peter coming back encouraged. Peter could see me, but it was not a conspicuous position to be observed by his peers.

However, on one occasion, his peers found it hard to accept Peter, and led him to go with them to a further point on the beach, and then very suddenly they ran away, and he was left alone, completely confused. As he felt at his lowest point, he looked up at the sand dunes, and Lionel was they're looking at him, and drew along side him. It was a touching moment, which led Peter to say "You-hoo". I realised that perhaps Lionel was aware of Peter's distress, or even if not, he was there at the right moment of time. There was a long emphasis to the word, but it showed the deep appreciation, which Peter had that he was not abandoned. Lionel then engaged with Peter on the beach, and sat near him, which he said meant an awful lot to him. Following this I felt the young person built up a sense of self-acceptance, enjoying throwing games with Lionel, and was still able to persevere, and meet these friends again. This has allowed him to maintain his self-confidence, and through staff, and his foster carers, guiding his strong imagination and storytelling ability, into drama and school productions with his peers, there has been positive interactions, which can only foster his ability to having meaningful friendships.

BULLYING

Another young person, whom I worked with, called Tom, was affected by witnessing violence towards his mother, from his father. However, he has a close and secure relationship with his mother, whom he lives with. His father was no longer living with them, though Tom had contact with him. Tom was referred because he was suffering from bullying at school, though his mother had previously been affected by alcohol, and Tom was concerned for her. Tom also had Kliens syndrome, with light sensitive skin.

I introduced Max and Jessie, to him, who had an immediate impact on Tom, and who warmed to him. We held many of the sessions in a local park, out of his locality, where certain children had been bullying him in the street. There seemed very few safe outlets for him. However, at the park, which was very popular with the public, he seemed to release a lot of tensions throwing the ball for Max and Jessie (stage one).

He also had a deeper experience, in one session, in which he sat flat on a merry go round, asking to be pushed lightly around, with Max watching. He looked with great focus in his eyes on the clouds in the sky, conveying a powerful sense, I felt, of 'why am I suffering as I am, is there any way out?' However through the gentle circular movement of the merry go round, along with a noticeable kick from him to keep it going too, and his focus on the clouds, his distress seemed to lessen. I reflected whether the expanse of something beyond himself-the clouds in the sky seemed to bring perspective, and strengthened him.

He also left the park on other occasions, when he challenged himself on balancing and climbing apparatus, more confident and empowered. This led to him gaining confidence to answer my questions verbally, and express his feelings concerning the issues of bullying and his relationships with his peers. Max was present in most sessions along with Jessie, and he always looked forward to seeing them. At the end of one of the sessions, with them he wanted to stay and stroke both of them, and gave them each 50 gentle touches counting precisely! This seemed very beneficial to him; he liked the touch contact with both dogs, speaking also of how soft the ears and head of Max were, which impacted him. It was interesting that it needed to be 50 for both dogs (stage two).

I felt Tom was gradually becoming more assertive, though there was still a fundamental blockage, which I couldn't seem to reach, within him, linked to how he saw himself. This I felt was the key to overcoming his bullying, even though he was now able to answer difficult children back, and feel better from this, along with handling himself better in the street. We had also engaged in role-plays, in which I would play the part of an aggressive neighbourhood peer, and Tom would be himself, and he would learn to speak back to them in a more assertive way. This seemed to empower him, and his mother mentioned he was getting more confident now.

Nevertheless, he still seemed unhappy within himself, and then suddenly at the end of one session, he looked behind to say goodbye to Max. He was quite sad, and didn't wish to go, and asked to stroke him. He kept stroking his head gently, which Max was happy with, and looked intently into Max's eyes. I was very aware we were just over his time limit of him being back in the house, though I felt I was witnessing something quite significant. I allowed this to continue, and the depth of feeling increased as he continued stroking Max, without any word being spoken (there was a special softness, to Max's head and ears). This was for over 5 minutes. Following this, Tom was happy to return to his home. This was a powerful sensory interaction. Immediately following this, in our subsequent sessions, Tom seemed much happier in himself. I felt the softness and unconditional acceptance of Max to Tom, and the warmth and affection, which Max showed towards him i.e. through his eyes, made a very significant impact on how Tom viewed him self now. It may have reached a deep childhood need, or absence, that may have been lacking for a long time in his life. It could also possibly have impacted a past trauma too (stage three).

In the sessions in the following year, after the summer break during which I sadly had to let Tom know that both Max and Jessie had tragically died,-and following the above interaction with Max, it began to emerge that Tom continued to be happier in himself. He was also continuing to get hassled less in the street, with less incidents of bullying at school, in which he reached the point of expressing, that he just looked at some of them and said don't be so stupid. The anxiety and worry lessened, and he made a successful re-integration into his primary school, and transition to his secondary school on visits.

While this was happening I introduced our new young Labrador, to Tom, who was very excited to meet Lionel. Amazingly, as he stroked Lionel straight away, he was happy for him to do this. Tom has Klien's syndrome, as mentioned above, with skin very sensitive to sunlight. He was also very sensitive to other people, and perhaps Lionel sensed this. Tom also spoke about not being happy about how he looked with freckles standing out on his face. I mentioned that freckles can go as you get older and many people have them, and suggested he re-frame his thinking, to 'many people have freckles and I'm ok'. He listened carefully, and I suggested that his view of himself and how he presents could allow other children to take advantage, which connected for the first time (stage four). Tom also asked, in subsequent sessions, to visit his local play park near his street, which showed a growth in confidence, and to have the opportunity to engage in some of the apparatus. This was where his bullies spent a lot of time. I was asked to walk a discreet distance behind, with Lionel, though close enough to quickly help if need be. Following this there were positive interactions with his peers, including some children who had previously been unkind to him, which was encouraging. I was allowed to support him on some of the apparatus too in future sessions.

Tom was also was showing more confidence in the street, and it seemed as if he had now unfrozen himself, to respond back to the unfairness of his peers (stage 5). This led to the other children in the street being keen to play with him. His credibility was growing. He was also keen to play with them, and was in a much more positive relationship with them now. He also spoke of his interest in art at school, affirmed by his mother, and spoke of wishing to join sea cadets (stage six)! I asked Tom, what he felt had made the difference to his life, and he said the climbing frames had really helped his confidence and our dogs.

Normality

One young person, Trevor (aged 9), had suffered from neglect and sexual abuse in his life, found real happiness in meeting Lionel, in our sessions. He had also been very angry, and unhappy in his life, feeling great uncertainty; it was very hard to place him in an appropriate setting. However, a foster placement was found in which he was really happy. The introduction of Lionel also integrated well with other approaches, which I used, all in the context of the seashore.

In our sessions, I worked on ways Trevor could be empowered using a beach environment. He was very keen to construct elaborate dams and waterways from the river running through the sands, along with bridges and harbours. Trevor felt a sense of purpose and direction through these constructions, and that he had achieved something in his life. His aim was to become an engineer when he grows up!

Another key aspect had been working as a team with myself, and exchanging communication through these constructions which was both co-operative, and gave opportunity for a positive outcome. The young person, for example, changed from one word exchanges, often ignoring my thoughts when we first met, to clear responses, thinking about what I said, in our later sessions. This would have a good balance, with him responding 'that's a good idea,' or 'thanks but it's better this way'. He also responded well to boundaries, which I applied concerning where we could and couldn't go on the beach.

However, when he met Lionel he had a real sense of joy, and would simply run and jump along the beach with him before we began our constructions, and throw a tennis ball, which Lionel would catch. Often while we working together, on the beach, Lionel would come close by and watch Trevor, who was always watchful if Lionel was ok. At the beginning of our sessions, when I collected Trevor from his foster family, he would look immediately in the car to see if Lionel was there, and at the end of the session, it became really important to him to be able to say goodbye to him. This was a special moment for Trevor, where he would stroke Lionel gently for a short time. This also provided a way in which he was happy to let go of our sessions, until we met again.

During an interim break in our sessions, when the authorities had to find the right foster placement for Trevor, he had asked about Lionel. It was commented by his Social Worker, that he had such a sparkle, when recalling his time with Lionel on the beach, which she hadn't seen in him before. It seemed to add an important ingredient into his life, of something happy to remember.

Therefore, there may be hidden benefits of animal therapy, which provide something hard to measure, but are simply creating experiences of normal enjoyment for young people who have suffered traumatic experiences.

Nurturing

Another young person, Billy (aged 9), who had additional needs, whom I worked with, was living with his grandparent where he was well cared for, settled, and happy in many respects. However, he also had experienced sadness and loss that he wasn't able to live with his mother, and receive the love, which he wished for from her. There was also a conflict between his grandparent and his mother, over who should be caring for him, and the level of contact, which his mother should be having with him, which could affect him. Any questions about his life were very stressful for him to respond to, and even when gently intonated, could cause him to feel angry or very depressed. On one occasion is response to a rare question from me, related to his feelings relating to his mother, he shouted very loudly 'shut-up'. He had been meeting with me twice weekly for up to one hour in his local school, for over 6 months, before I asked the question.

Billy found it very hard to settle at school with those uncertainties, and express to any one how he was really feeling. Whenever there was a home difficulty, this could affect his behaviour at school, and he could become very angry. However, he had a strong interest in rabbits, which he kept as pets at home.

One of the ways he felt able to express himself in our sessions (I worked with him for 4 years) was through drawing his favourite rabbits, whom he was very fond of. He enjoyed drawing their various expressions in a special A4 size scrapbook, which I kept for him. The drawings, in which Billy used different coloured pastels, often showed the rabbits as large creatures with very expressive eyes, and ears, with large teeth, (stage 1).

However, they also allowed him to focus on his home life in a very safe way, for him. They included Billy taking one of the rabbits for a walk to the park in a harness, going through a tunnel in the park, and entering its own cage at home. Billy was also able to describe his rabbits, with the number of teeth, which they had, or their whiskers, and show when they were smiling (stages 1/2).

He also found it very empowering to express himself in this way, often showing a sparkle of humour about the rabbits trying to escape at home! As he progressed in confidence, over a period of a year, he was able to express verbally that, his favourite rabbit "gives me a lot of love", which was a valuable breakthrough time for him, and reflected the significance of his rabbits to him (stage 2).

There is a softness and warmth to rabbits, in which they can be hugged, and provide something very special, to young people, especially if they have been missing this, nurturing aspect from their early life. With Billy, this often became apparent, when he would move into a phase of silence, separated even from myself in the interaction of our session, focused into the inner pain of his life, though with gently re-focusing he came out of it, and the frequency lessened in time.

One of the ways I used to facilitate this re-focusing, along with discussion of his rabbits, was through introducing Lionel, who became a constant encouragement to Billy, particularly if there was anything naughty, which he had done! This provided humour, which was a valuable strategy, in strengthening him, out of tough situations, and led to him asking focused questions about 'what' Lionel had done. When I explained it was through, for example, cream cakes being pinched, or bread being very skilfully taken from a kitchen worktop, he would really laugh, and this could set a positive tone for the whole session.

As Billy felt more confident, I saw him in home situations, and he would always ask to take Lionel out for a walk. This became one of his main focuses, and developed a confidence for him in going into more public situations, which otherwise he may not have been able to do. Alongside this, he would be very keen to care for Lionel. A priority would be safely seeing him out of the car from the pavement onto the park field, throwing the ball for him, and observing when he was tired or very hot, in which case Billy would ask if we could return to the car because of Lionel's needs.

At this point, he would always give him water in the boot of the car, and a great joy for him would be giving Lionel space-he was aware that he was very shy if being watched and being able to 'hear' Lionel lap up the water (stage 3). This sensory aspect of sound particularly, had a very positive impact on Billy, who would in a very excited manner, when hearing the actual lapping sound, say to me, 'he's drinking, he's drinking (stage 4)'. He was communicating, how important this was to him. There was a sense of Billy, knowing that he had done something good, and was caring or making a difference to Lionel's life, accompanied by a huge smile on his face. He may have suffered enormously (guilt) from feeling that he hadn't been able to do this for his mother, or for other members of his family, though at the same time, he would see I had overall responsibility for Lionel. I explained to him on some occasions, for example, that it was too hot or too wet to bring Lionel, which he accepted (stage 5).

This structure, brought a routine sense of security for Billy, which seemed valuable to him, and also allowed him to build up a lot more self-confidence, and alongside the support of secondary school staff, his family, and other professionals, enabled him to adjust to secondary education in a phased manner, successfully (towards stage 6). He also had joined cubs, achieving awards, and more recently was showing interest in other groups such as army cadets.

I also reflected whether the caring and love which Billy was showing to Lionel was a way he was self-learning, through this process of nurturing for Lionel, about what he needed to do to fill a gap in his own life. In other words, emotionally this was naturally happening, like a regression, to what he may not have had at an early age, before allowing him to then move forwards in his life. Also that this process could equip him, along side the care he was getting from his family and school, with the awareness and skills that he needs to care for others when he is older. The emerging sense of this consideration arose from the naturalness in which Billy engaged in the care process for Lionel, as if it was a part of what 'needed to be'.

EMPOWERMENT

The last theme relates to Josh (aged 10), who with his younger brother witnessed violence to his mother from his stepfather. He had mild Aspergus Syndrome, and was also experiencing bullying from two peers at school, over a sustained period of time. This made him feel very angry, and he found that by releasing his tensions on climbing apparatus in a local park, and overcoming his fear of heights, he gained a lot of self-confidence, to be able to talk about difficult situations at school. This focused on two peers in his class, one of whom hit Josh's head against a school desk. Josh, had originally felt the best way of handling this was by hiding in a special nature den during school playtimes, away from the children who made his life a misery, with a constant sense of threat coming, which he had to be alert to, and respond to by 'flight'.

However, as he overcame his fear of heights on the climbing apparatus, these reactions lessened, and he stood his ground against these bullies more at school, causing them to run off. There were still conflicts, but Josh was able to give back more, and the issues then changed to guidance about handling this appropriately without hurting back. There was also the resonance of the violence which he had seen in his home to his mother, making the school issues much more significant to him, and threatening. Josh also saw things in a logical way, though when I asked him about painful areas such as his feelings about the violence he witnessed, he responded to me, 'I do not want to talk about this'.

However, I introduced Max and Jessie, into some of our sessions, whom he really liked, and it prompted him to talk about his own dog, whom he used to have at home with his mum and step dad, but who, he said, had to go to a better place, which he called 'dog heaven'. This led to him saying that his dog was hiding under the bed when the police came, when his mum and step dad split up, and it was at night, and he had to call his dog to come down and go with them, otherwise he would have been left there for many days. This was the first time he had been able to share anything about this traumatic experience in his home.

On a further session, I brought Max, and after walking along a riverside, which had a peaceful therapeutic atmosphere, Josh felt able to speak again about his dog, whom he said had a choice of going to another place or a farm. Josh added that he felt it would be best for his dog to stay on a farm where he could run around, and this was what happened. I then recalled to Josh that he spoke previously about remembering that his dog was hiding upstairs under a bed, when the police arrived at night, and he then felt able to say in this session, that he called his dog from downstairs and then he came down.

As we were talking, we paused by some picnic tables, and I sensed for the first time that Josh wished to talk further, and was very happy that Max was sat down nearby. As I asked him if he heard his mother being hurt, or saw it, he started watching Max, and walking around the picnic tables, which he continued to do, while we talked. This was quite remarkable, as he continued his eye contact on Max, sharing in response to my question, that he was there and that his mother came back, and he saw blood by the switch. The tone of something she said, seemed to impact him, and he went on to say, while continuing to walk around the picnic table with his eyes on Max, that he was upstairs reassuring his younger brother by his bed, and that he had to scream at his brother to keep quiet. This seemed the key pressure point, which he released. He was then able to express his feelings saying that he felt sad for his mother and angry and sad for his step dad.

In a later session, he shared that he had moved on from this traumatic experience, and that talking had helped him to do this, and that he found it easier to talk when our dogs were there. Although there was a further incident involving his peers, Josh spoke of responding back verbally to them without running away or hitting back at them, and that he was looking forwards to his maths SATs exam. There may have been some jealousy from some of his peers towards him too, as he was quite able with maths. He also in a further session, spoke about his birth father for the first time, and when he sees him, sharing insights about his life, and the life of his own grandparents whom he stayed with, when having to leave his family home. He was also able to see his step dad, who was not with his mother any more, and go on holiday with him and his younger brother, in the future, and reflected that along with seeing the dogs he found the climbing apparatus the most helpful experiences. His mother also felt able to listen to his feelings and thoughts at home.

Overall, I felt Josh had been able to move forwards in his life now, and was much more self-confident and empowered both at school, and at home, from his experiences on the climbing frames, and from being able to talk about his past trauma, with the help of Max and Jessie in our sessions.

The intervention of animals therefore can make an important contribution into traumatised young people's lives. As well as showing narrative evidence, there may be opportunities for those in the psychological professions to develop quantifiable criteria evidencing possible change though the intervention of animals. This could relate to future costing challenges to justify this approach. One example of a way forward is the six stage approach of animal therapy focused on in this section, with a number matching each criteria that a young person reaches through animal therapy.

Conclusion

In conclusion, the five sections simply reflect four different approaches in environmental therapy, which can be applied independently, or inter-related, to help traumatised young people come to terms with traumatic events in their lives, and both restore and empower them for their future lives.

Using a specific environment, such as the sea shore or the park can allow young people to approach very painful events safely and with confidence to express their true feelings, and feel empowered through enactments in these environments. There are many other environments that can be chosen through open and creative thinking' whether the therapist is working in a rural or urban location. The key aspect is connecting with the young person in a child centred way so that they can feel comfortable to express themselves in therapeutic sessions.

The therapist needs to engage with this, provided he is happy that it fulfils both his sense of feeling 'ok' about working in a specific environment, and that it is safe. Following this, preparation to evaluate the environment before the sessions begin is very good practice.

Allowing the young person to choose the environments which they wish to use for their therapeutic sessions, is another approach which can be very effective, through them engaging in environments which they are comfortable in culturally, and which link with past traumatic events. This can facilitate very open identification with an abusive past, with a supportive therapist alongside them. This approach can be challenging, but it gives a clear signal to the young person that 'they are being heard', and can allow their life story or narrative to unfold, profoundly, and can help them to re-visit their deepest areas of pain safely. This can give a normalising sense to the client, and then allow the most repressed areas of experience to be released, within a safe and positive context. In the above case study, the family Inn became the main environment where the client felt able to re-live his past, and then move forwards in his life to a place of self-acceptance. Recently, I worked using this approach - to help a young person who had suffered traumatic peer abuse-, who chose his local (urban) street environment, open sand dunes by the sea which he frequently went to, and an indoor skate park to process what happened to him and move forwards in his life. However, perhaps most impactful for him was in his time of greatest distress my dog, just sat down alongside him whilst outdoors by the sea dunes and was 'with him'. Therefore, different environmental approaches can be combined too.

A more directive approach within outdoor skills, such as canoeing, can positively affect the self-esteem of a young person. With this way of using the outdoor environment, a more guided and mentoring approach, can be just what a young person who has lacked this in his earlier life needs, rather than a pure child centred approach. The key aspect for this to work successfully, and be a valuable therapeutic experience, is to use the skill focus to build self-confidence, while at the same time allowing space for the client to express himself therapeutically, and have choice within this context. This worked above with a young person who was keen to achieve his one star award, but who also wished to stop and just feel the water and look at the clouds, which had powerful symbolic and sensory significance for him. Following this, he was able to re-focus on his skills with renewed energy.

The final approach using animal therapy, I found, was very effective with young people who found verbal dialogue too difficult to handle, and who needed more of a sensory and interactive approach. This related to engaging with our dogs in a practical way involving touch, and other senses, particularly sight, where the look of the dogs eyes became very important. This gave the opportunity for the young people, to identify through contact with Max, Jessie, or Lionel, with something, which they were missing in their life, and needed to identify with when it was otherwise very difficult to express. This connected with some of the young people I worked with, with a lack of closeness or attachment to their mothers, which they felt a great gap from, and found painful. This affected their relationships with others. Some had special needs, and found it very hard to voice their pain, or even know how to express it. The use of animals, and for me using my dogs, allowed an interaction of love which somehow reached into this absence, and gave them a sense of being able to both give love and receive love unconditionally which meant so much to them. It began to allow them for the first time to accept themselves and move forwards in their lives.

Appendix One:
Recognising the Affect of Abuse

Children and young people who have been subject to abuse, whether sexual, physical, emotional, or neglect, experience trauma which profoundly damages their lives, resulting in them needing therapeutic help. They may also experience stress, which could be either at the time of the abuse, or delayed over a period of months or even years. This is called Post Traumatic Stress.

There are 5 key non-verbal signs of Post Traumatic Stress, amongst younger children (Fredrick; 1985).

1.) Doubts about self, including comments about their body, self-worth, and a possible desire to withdraw.
2.) Conduct disturbances, related to anxiety and uncertainty, at home and school.
3.) Separation anxiety or clinging behaviour. This could relate to not wishing to return to school.
4.) Sleep disturbances over a period of time, in which dreams of the trauma could occur.
5.) Phobias about disturbing stimuli that remind the victim of the traumatic event e.g. TV scenes.

Other key symptoms of abuse, for young people of all ages, found from a study by Martin and Beezley (1977), included:

1.) Psychosomatic stress symptoms including bed wetting, eating problems, and compulsive issues, or rituals e.g. personal cleanliness over their hands.
2.) Low self-esteem.

3.) Lack of concentration at school.
4.) Impaired capacity to enjoy life e.g. pre-occupied, unsettled.
5.) Withdrawal. Finding it difficult to relate to peers and becoming isolated.
6.) Depression.
7.) Defiance. Showing a negative or confrontational approach, or being unco-operative.
8.) Hyper-vigilance.
9.) Pretence of security e.g. appearance of being very good all the time or capable and independent. Also, showing indiscriminate affection to any adult who gives them attention.
10.) Unaware of the feelings of others who they may affect, or lack of sensitivity to others.

BIBLIOGRAPHY

Cattanach, A. (2008)
Play Therapy with Abused Children.
London: Jessica Kingsley.

Culley, S. and Bond, T. (2004)
Integrative Counselling Skills in Action.
London: Sage.

Rowland, N. and Goss, S.
(2000) *Evidence-Based Counselling and psychological Therapies.*
London: Routledge.

Woskett, V. (1999)
The Therapeutic Use of self.
London: Routledge.

Mearns, D. and Thorne, B. (1998)
Person-Centred Counselling In Action.
London: Sage.

De Board, R. (1998)
Counselling For Toads.
London: Routledge (TA approach).

Altman, R. (1996)
Through the Counselling Maze.
Eastbourne: Kingsway.

www.ingramcontent.com/pod-product-compliance
Lightning Source LLC
Chambersburg PA
CBHW020502030426
42337CB00011B/194